A DREAM OF PARIS

A Personal Travel Memoir

Neal Atherton

Neal Atherton
French Travel Write

To all the friends and family that have shared the most treasured times in Paris - Until we meet again

CONTENTS

PHOTOGRAPHY

**Please enjoy some extra photography
from our travels in Paris**

On my Website: PARIS PHOTOGRAPHY

All Available on Amazon for Kindle & Unlimited

NEW BOOK July 8th 2022

A DREAM OF PARIS

Writing this book has been more personal than I would have expected. My first two books about travels in the South of France were obviously personal in the sense that we were the ones that experienced the events in those books. Essentially though they were travelogues or travel memoirs. Recalling our many visits to Paris was much more than a mere travel journey. I came to realise just how much the city means to me and more importantly the value of our friends. I think that I do have to explain why we ever went to Paris at all and why it came to have so much significance. Paris, that most beautiful of cities, means so much to me because of all the moments spent there with friends. Gaining so many memories that are still fresh and vibrant and with the passage of time have not faded or altered at all. Our love of the city is undiminished and we still find new and exciting people and places on each visit. So that is the easy part of the explanation.

Why did we begin to travel to Paris at all? The first time was back in 1997, just weeks before Princess Diana's tragic death. If you have read my first book on Amazon - 'First time we Saw Paris' - you will know that our first visit to Paris was a fleeting one, late in the evening and in darkness, a passing through over which we had no control of the itinerary. It was magical certainly but why did we return to discover Paris for ourselves? I thought for quite a while about that. Finally I realised that the main influence on me as to why I travelled to discover Paris were the words of Joni Mitchell. Possibly this was a subliminal effect over many years but it was a feeling that would not go away, even in the years when I was determined to be a lifelong stay at home tourist. I would go only as far as the English coastline would allow my car to travel before falling into the sea.

Now, American or Canadian writers use the names of towns and cities to great romantic and imaginative effect. They make them sound so cinematic and vivid, conjuring up a vision; a movie in our imagination. Somehow English place names just don't cut it. Emmylou's 'Boulder to Birmingham' tells a story, somehow 'Milton Keynes to Hull' just doesn't do it for me. However I still have no desire to visit the New Jersey Turnpike but it does stir the imagination. Joni's treatment of Paris entered into my mind on a different level.

I remember how from first hearing 'California' the words where she describes being in the Paris park reading the news - the lyric gave me an immediate feeling about the city. The atmosphere that it would show to me stayed with me over the years. From those few words I could visualize the park and ultimately for me that came to be the Tuileries and the green metal chairs scattered around the ponds. Seared on my brain was her word picture, simple, sparse and economical.

In the 1990's when work was a much more serious affair and responsibilities so much greater, when the working week never really ended but you were always available - then I really understood Joni's song 'Free

Man in Paris':

I wanted that freedom - I wanted to feel that no one would call me and I could enjoy the feeling of not being found.

She gave the sense that to just give it all up and wander the Paris streets and cafes was exactly the thing to do.

The 'I' in the song of course was David Geffen but when I heard that lyric then it was ME and I wanted that freedom.

At that time in my life I only had to listen to those lyrics and feel that I just had to go and experience Paris. No phones, no contact with anyone but have some freedom and explore Paris. Ultimately that is why we went and that is what we did. Please enjoy Paris and make it your own and if you are unsure just listen to a song or two of Joni Mitchell.

Yes, these writings are personal and they will convey my deep affection for Paris and the friends and family with whom we have shared these times together. However, I have tried at times to step back from that process. In the writing of the book I have also included some thoughts and information on various places, restaurants and historical aspects of the city.

For me it is essential to look at Paris with an open and curious mind. It is true that the Eiffel Tower has to be seen and of course you cannot miss it unless you are on it, but there is so very much more to be absorbed. I hope you enjoy the pointers in the book and it encourages you to discover more and make Paris a deeper and richer experience. With a little effort and research you will reap the rewards.

Some places, people and events will occur more than once in the book and that was essential to tell the stories surrounding them. It will also emphasize that these are to me especially important and I hope you will agree.

So please enjoy this book - it is part journal, partly informative, it has historical moments . What it does have is my love of the city and the people I met or travelled with. I trust that love shines through.

One thing I have spent many hours mulling over and sought plenty of advice on is the titles to give to my books. I have two books on Amazon – 'First Time we Saw Paris' and 'Thyme for Provence'. Naming them was torturous and even now I am not sure I am content with the final results. This latest book is about our times in Paris over a period of many years. Paris travel is so familiar and enjoyable that I thought writing it would be straightforward. It was not and I think that familiarity and how much my life and times in Paris mean to me caused the writing problem - but I got there. One thing about this book that has turned out to be easy is the title and for that I have to thank my treasured granddaughter - Ronelle.

For me writing this Paris travel book in this particular year has special meaning. Earlier this year we lost the dearest of friends. She was a unique irreplaceable person with whom we often travelled and shared so many wonderful times in Paris. June was the organizer, the glue that held our party together and the most generous of souls. We loved her so much. Young Ronelle knew this. Even though she was only six years old she knew our sadness and also our pleasure in recalling June. So the young artist drew the attached picture for us. She had picked up from our conversations that Paris was our uniquely special place and she themed her beautiful tribute on the city. I am second from the right and curly haired June is fourth. It is a picture of pure joy and of course hope.

The title is hers - A DREAM OF PARIS - how simple and concise and how so very appropriate and perfect. So even though the book took a while to be finished I surely had my title from the very start.

THE FIRST TIME
WE SAW PARIS

Our first encounter with Paris was in 1997 and I have told the full story about that evening in my debut book 'The First Time We Saw Paris'. For the context of this book I will briefly recount that first voyage into the unknown.

That initial experience of Paris was as a pleasant detour on a journey by coach from the North of England as we were out-bound to a holiday at Canet Plage, a coastal town close to Perpignan in the Catalan region of south west France. The stay in Paris would only be for around one and a half hours but it would have a huge impact on me. It would reinforce that this all too fleeting visit would not be the last. As we sped down the autoroute towards the suburbs of Paris this was the very first time I had actually left the shores of England. Everything I was seeing was fresh to my eyes but I appreciate that for many who may be reading this and also for a good number on the coach it was all very familiar. My travel upbringing had been very conservative and it was only in recent years that I had gone as far as taking my family to Devon and Cornwall for our holidays. Even that seemed like a very long way to me. This passing through Paris was an exploration in comparison to my limited travel destinations.

We passed Charles de Gaulle Airport as a four engined jet plane took off and away. It seemed impossibly close to our coach as it rose over the road in front of us. We also viewed the State de France skeleton of a stadium - it being under construction for the soccer world cup in the following year. I would so love to have been back for that tournament.

As a first time visitor it was an undoubted thrill to see the city unfold in front of me as we emerged from the unattractive suburbs. Coming into view was the brightly lit hill of Montmartre with Sacre Coeur at its heart (sorry). This view conjures up in my mind the picture (sorry again) of so many artists working and living on those streets. These artists I had grown to love as my cultural education progressed.

Soon we were right in the centre of the action of this vibrant city and trying to negotiate the Place Charles de Gaulle. Also known as Place de l'Étoile, this roadway circles around the Arc de Triomphe. As I look down from the window of the coach I see cars at right angles to our vehicle. The drivers are manic, seemingly deranged as they form a disorderly scrum of traffic, all trying to reach one of the exits on this star- shaped arena.

It is when we finally reach our exit at the very top of the Champs-Élysées that I get a breath-taking view down the boulevard. On reaching the Place de la Concorde we are at last able to stop and set foot on the streets of Paris, French soil, trying to take it all in. For some on the coach this is just another cigarette break and that saddens me. I am like an enthralled young child and always will be when I can spend time in the Place de la Concorde. On other visits we will discover a particular favourite location just across the way – Le Jardins de Tuileries.

I suppose in a way my reaction to these places that I have never seen before in the flesh - the Eiffel Tower, Maxim's, Place Vendome & the Paris Ritz, Notre

Dame and others is as if I am still a wide-eyed innocent child. Never having travelled out of England despite reaching such an advanced age as 42 it all appears so exciting and especially so to be sharing it with my children. Even though the visit is only for just over an hour it does form a bond with the sights and sounds of Paris. These bonds will endure and ensure that we do return to experience the city to the full.

Also in retrospect this has been an important time to be in Paris. Shortly afterwards on another balmy Paris night Princess Diana was involved in her fatal crash. It was a strange feeling to have taken that very same route on this short guided tour.

We soon headed out of Paris and on to our holiday in the south but we had formed a lasting attachment to Paris. We would return the following year as a family. That next trip would be a starter in our love of Paris but was again quite a short break.

Although it would be a very happy and enjoyable time with the family, I was coming to realize that there was more to Paris than any other city, including London, that I had visited in the past. I have always had a great love of history and my research and brief forays into Paris had opened up a very interesting world of exploration that I was keen to immerse myself in. I had developed a particular fascination with the events during the Second World War occupation of the city. Also, coupled with the time of the liberation of Paris I realised there was much to discover and I was keen to do so.

You may of course appreciate that a young family may not be quite so inclined to be lectured about the life and times of the history of Paris. It was really only on the next few trips without children that I started to really discover and understand . It is a city that gives so much if you are prepared to make the effort and I was like a sponge in soaking up everything that it had to offer.

The trip with the family offered many memories that have been treasured. My son James had in fact already been to Paris a few months earlier with his college friends as part of the photography course he was pursuing. He did not tell me very much about what he saw and perhaps it was best not to ask.

He did come back with some wonderful black and white photos, revealing that he had met Sharon Stone on a photoshoot by the Eiffel Tower. His teenage eyes were not really in tune with mine however. Even so, as he had been before I demurred to let him be the tour guide on our visit. I had lots of places I wished to visit and my developing love of food and cookery was edging me towards some foodie experiences.

He had his culinary taste buds set on the Hard Rock Café. James took us there one evening as he informed us that he had been there before. It was very much to our amusement that he could not find it despite his youthful confidence in his navigation skills. It was only when I pointed out that it just might be the building with the brightly lit 'Hard Rock Café' sign beaming out into the street that he finally got his bearings. Needless to say I still remind him of that.

Charlotte too had her moment of embarrassment on the Champs-Élysées although she easily brushed this one off and left me to deal with it. We were strolling past Fouquet's famous red fronted restaurant, its terrace lively with contented diners.

As we meandered by, a young man proffered a single red rose which she gladly accepted. Now Charlotte being a not unattractive young lady to say the least, felt that it was a quite natural thing to have been given. She carried on walking and proudly held the attractive rose as she did so. It was only after we had walked a couple of blocks that the young man cut in front of me and blocked my progress, talking quickly and animatedly in French. I eventually gathered that his noble gesture with the red rose was not a romantic one but purely a financial transaction and he expected payment. On balance it seemed handing over a few francs was the best way out of this situation and the most expensive single stem rose in the world was paid for and Charlotte carried on obliviously up the Champs-Élysées.

All in all it was a very enjoyable trip and excellent time together as a family in what for us was a completely different setting. For myself though I knew there was more to Paris and that I must return to take the city on another level. I would do that extensively and with great joy.

On that family trip we ended with a close encounter with a famous Frenchman. In fact he was exceptionally famous in that particular year as a French footballer who had played a large part in the country winning the soccer world cup in Paris just a few weeks earlier. The Gare du Nord was incredibly hot today, with precious little air wafting through the station.

My wife was hoping for a seat as we awaited the Eurostar to London. We stood close to an occupied seat at which sat a giant of a man, immaculately dressed in a well-tailored suit and expensive accessories. He very kindly stood up and allowed Niamh to sit down and as he wandered off I followed him for a short distance. I knew who he was, he was heading back to his club in London on the same train as ourselves. I should have had the confidence to approach him and thank him and also congratulate him on his thrilling accomplishments; sadly my English reserve kicked in. I am pleased to say that this 'reserve' no longer exists. Some years later this gentleman was on TV as a pundit at a French world cup soccer game and Niamh was watching. I was cooking in the kitchen but looked in to announce that she had previously met this man. With just a very little prompting she pinpointed the time she had met him and remembered his gentlemanly gesture. That was a lovely memory and one that I had kept in reserve to that moment – a bit of fun.

So, what did I find in Paris sans children. Let us see and I do hope you will be inspired to go and to make your own memories in this most wonderful of cities. Yes, please dream of Paris but do act on it and experience the city for yourself.

Chapter End Photos courtesy of Ben Atherton

CAFÉ MED

I have genuinely always wanted to experience a Michelin starred dining experience in Paris but so far on my many travels here I have never got around to doing so. I love cooking, searching out excellent  produce and sourcing exceptional wines from vineyards around the regions of France. Therefore it is natural that I would love to try something that aspires to the highest levels of cooking using the finest of French produce. The restaurant I have always had my eye on visiting is the venerable Le Grand Véfour in the arcades of the Palais-Royal; Napoleon and Josephine's local eatery of choice. I have looked at the menu posted at the door and peered enviously inside but up to now that is as far as the experience has developed.

You see, the problem is that when you are in Paris for only three or four days you will always find so many places to eat that will draw you inexorably inside. There are far more restaurants and cafes than you can possibly patronize in the time available. Although I do not consider myself to be tight-fisted, these chosen places tend to be a little more humble in their pretensions. I love going somewhere that gives an experience that is far greater than the sum of its parts. Paris is full of such establishments.

This is a story of one such restaurant that is a place that draws us back on every trip. It also highlights what is so fine about travelling in France and Paris in particular – there is always somewhere that you take your friends and leave you with incomparable memories. These memories will continue to be shared and re-lived years later. Let me take you back to a particular day in the early part of the new millennium.

I will refer to Café Med at 77 Rue Saint-Louis en l'Île on other occasions in my writing but on this day it was the central point in a memorable day we spent with dear friends. Our party of fourteen or so (who's counting) had gone in two different directions. Four had decided to have the Michelin starred experience at a restaurant close to the river. They were then to go on to the Palais Garnier opera house for a tour of the famous building. The rest of us had a lovely stroll along the Seine and ended up at Café Med for lunch. Madam found or should I say constructed for us a long table at the back of the restaurant which just about accommodated us all.

We settled down to a very, and I do mean very, convivial lunch. Café Med serves three menus of limited choice but set at varied price points. None of these will set you back any more than a modest starter at one of Paris' fine dining venues. The food comes down to the restaurant via a dumb waiter from what must be a tiny kitchen located above the small bar. Service is always performed with great efficiency and everything is brought to your table fresh, ideal for locals on their lunch break. We however, it must be said, were in no rush and Madam was happy to pace our meal to be in line with our wine consumption.

Can I just say at this point that they do the finest sautéed potatoes in all of France and alongside a thin entrecote steak it makes the most perfect of main courses for lunch. Anyway this part is not a food review really but I had to say it.

Our friend Des, despite the close proximity of his wife, has struck up a repartee with Madam that has all the makings of a fine double act. Or perhaps the possibility of him never coming home with us at all. Despite coming across as

very much the lady in charge, seemingly aloof and not to be messed with, she engages with her clientele effortlessly. However, you do sense that you must still know your place.

Des has broken through any perceived haughty exterior and he is unstoppable. I do sense that what may stop him is a carafe of wine being poured over his head by Natasha, his wife. Thankfully she knows him well enough to allow him his little flirtation and it is entertaining our table not to mention everyone else in the restaurant. A vital component of places like this is that they have to provide excellent people watching and Café Med does that in bucket loads. On this occasion we are probably the ones being watched.

We finally get towards the end of our meal but

are still looking to call Madam over to get a couple more carafes of their lovely rosé house wine. Joan then announces that we are actually due to meet up with the rest of the party at the Garnier Opera house in around 20 minutes or so. Really, that was news to the rest of us . We were so settled. So much so in fact that we had lined up all the wine glasses along two sides of the table and got our host to take a photo of the group of us and the residue of our most agreeable lunch.

But Joan, who is unquestionably the one in charge of our party is insistent that we move on and vacate the scene. We all stumble out saying our goodbyes to all in the restaurant, leave generous tips, and Des gets the hug he was longing for.

We start to plot the quickest route to the Opera house. We start by going the wrong way along the island though and then realize that to get to the nearest Metro we have to go back along the banks of the river the full length again of Ile Saint-Louis. Eventually we are able to end the footslogging and start the journey. From a truly tranquil state in the restaurant we are now all sweating and bedraggled as we pile into the metro carriage deep underground. The train takes us close to the Opera House and we emerge back into daylight.

None of us are really up to this visit and

certainly from our appearance must stand a fair chance of being refused admission. The accommodating lady on the door does allow us access and we head up the Grand Escalier with its multi coloured marble. We take the right side of the dual staircase to make our way to the surrounds of the magnificent auditorium itself. The entrances to the various boxes take your imagination back to elegant times past and we open a doorway that gives us a full panoramic view of this breath-taking theatre. It is all too much to take in after a long leisurely lunch and we still have not found our friends.

At that point we hear a familiar distant cackle of laughter and looking down from on high we spot them as distant specks in front of the stage. They are taking part in a guided tour. There is no possibility of reaching them, not in our condition of desperately needing a siesta and even Joan realises the game is up and gives us permission to retrace our steps to the Metro station which we gratefully do. We still have to go out again tonight as we have a special meal booked but room service and a sandwich would surely be the sensible option.

Showered, spruced up and eyes propped open we gather in the foyer of the hotel once again and make our way to Restaurant Marie-Edith which fortunately is a mere stones throw across the road. Even then this walk is quite far enough. This was a must do restaurant for James in our party and his culinary reputation depends on it delivering satisfaction such is his enthusiasm for the place and his insistence that we all eat there.

He has no need to worry as this is a wonderful place to eat, very Parisian, all wood film set Belle Époque panelling outside, crisp white tablecloths, zinc topped wooden bar and very fine food and wine. One member of our party is sadly missing in action. Henry, who had desired the Michelin star meal rather than our more humble fare, was back in his room within easy distance of the bathroom, struck down by food poisoning. We chose our lunch well, I thought smugly. The meal tonight is so, so good and the service quintessentially French - perfectly judged. We remain on our best behaviour and savour the moment.

Our possible descent into silliness is only briefly threatened when I am asked to order another bottle of wine, - me being the French wine expert and all that. Des, Richard and I agree to split the cost of a fine bottle of red between us. Richard is unaware of the cost of my choice. Des is not and can barely contain himself thinking of the reaction of Richard when he has to provide the contents of his wallet. Before that Richard is profuse in his expressions of joy at just what the French can extract from a few choice grapes, blissfully unaware that each mouthful is costing him more than a bottle of his usual plonk back home.

Also at this point Richard has chosen his dessert. The waiter is informing him in the most exaggerated Anglo/French that there is a 'supplement' for this particular choice. Des and Richard cannot resist imitating the waiter's 'supel – aye – mo-aant' for several minutes until I have to tell them to shut up before we are thrown out. It is still repeated down to this day in any restaurant we find ourselves in – even McDonalds.

The restaurant is extremely good, a fine choice but James was so persuasive with us – excessively so - that we had to dine here. Why was that? It all becomes clear as the dessert is served. It is the finest, yes undoubtedly the finest Îles flottantes (floating islands) known to man. This is THE dessert for James, the very pinnacle of his culinary delight. That is why he has brought us here. We still talk about it many years later, this extraordinary example of the pastry chef's art. I doff my cap in appreciation and bow the head – one of the finest things I have eaten.

What a day, a day of friendship and shared experiences, mainly culinary.

Café Med – well it is a fixture in our travels to Paris.

Yes I would one day love a Michelin starred experience but as I am always going to have to choose between Café Med or the three coveted stars there will always only be time for the one winner.

HEMINGWAY,
MIDNIGHT IN PARIS
AND A TASTE
OF HISTORY

One of the most evocative books about Paris could be considered to be Ernest Hemingway's 'A Moveable Feast'. If ever I need inspiration to write  about Paris or to make plans for another visit then that is the book that clinches my mood and motivation. It works every time for me even though you do have to take some of his Paris memoir writing with a large pinch of salt. He paints such insightful but sometimes harshly unsympathetic portraits of the characters from the era. Portraits of the writers and artists that dominated '20s Paris. Describing so well the life and ambiance of the city of that time period – he constructs a painting in words.

His portrait of F Scott Fitzgerald made me laugh, cry and wince at the astonishingly eccentric tales he recalled.

Yet it is a book that has such a depth of sadness too. Like my taste in music it appeals to my melancholic side – as my daughter says; 'the sadder the better'. Certainly there is a sadness surrounding the future aftermath of Fitzgerald's and his wife Zelda's tragically short lives. Lives that spiralled downhill shortly after these events. It is though the final chapter of a book that was written just before Hemingway's lonely death nearly forty years detached in time from the events in the book that conveys his deep regret. He threw away the happiness of his life in Paris with his first wife Hadley and their young son. There is not always something better around the corner, often what we already have is all we need for our contentment.

It is a book that can be a Parisian guide but today we have something more visual based on his work.

The Woody Allen film 'Midnight in Paris' is

themed on Hemingway's book as any cursory read of it will establish. Really though it is a film that does more for the Paris tourist board than any amount of advertising. It is a love letter to a great city. The film recreates the times of the 20's that Hemingway so eloquently describes, an era that the film's main character Gil adores as he is bewilderingly entranced to be transported back to that time. Adriana, his new muse, prefers La Belle Époque but he cannot understand wanting anything more than to be experiencing the lively writing and arts scene of Paris in the 20's. I am with him on that, but really all the book and the movie do is to convince you that Paris is the finest city in the world. When I arrive at the Gare Du Nord on the Eurostar from London then my current era waiting outside the station is just fine by me.

The filming locations for 'Midnight in Paris' are well documented and in fact Hemingway makes a fine job of that. So if you want to follow them all it is easy to do so in our smartphone era. I will take you through on a mixed journey, some of the places in the film that I love. I will also bring in some parts of Paris that historically are so very interesting and should be part of your visit. If your time in Paris is all fine dining then you are missing out on a broader experience.

If you are going to start on a history and writing tour of Paris then I suggest it begins on the steps of the church of St Etienne du Mont, Place Sainte-Geneviève, 75005. These, the actual steps used in the film where Gil waits for the time travelling car and his famous host, are just around to the side of the church. From here they look down Rue de la Montagne Sainte Geneviève, the road where the car approaches. It is a supremely evocative location and it is worth taking the time to search out on the internet a photo taken on 22nd August 1944 of armed resistants just coming down from the area of the steps at the height of the struggle to liberate Paris from the German occupiers. Historical fact and fiction can be found being enacted side by side on the streets of Paris and in your imagination.

If you go back around to the front of the church on to Rue Clovis and then head towards the Latin Quarter by turning right onto Rue Descartes you will come to a small but perfectly formed restaurant - La Maison de Verlaine. The clue is in the title but it was not a happy place when Verlaine died there in a miserable state as a result of his alcoholism. It is also a building where Hemingway rented a small attic room and took himself off to write in peace and seclusion. There is a delightful story in his book about the goatherd taking his flock every day past Hemingway's building and milking his goats to order as the locals emerged with their containers. It is certainly an evocative street. We have eaten on the terrace at this restaurant of an evening and the food is excellent. The location is pure Paris left bank so don't let me stop you going. Just a little farther up is Place Contrescarpe which again features in Hemingway's life and times in Paris. This is a place where he describes almost with affection the bar humming with the pungent smell of bodies and drunkenness. It is a vivid portrait you can almost sense the reality of from the page.

Today it is a lively square and to sit and eat at a table (we ate overly large portions of Greek food one night at L'Ile de Crete) gives you quite a show as life quite literally revolves around you. It is a place that is perfect for riding a motorbike around and around or posing in an open topped car. A ready supply of onlookers at the cafes and bars will either admire you or stare in total disdain.

Around the corner at 74 Rue Cardinal Lemoine is the building that houses the small apartment that the Hemingways lived in from 1922. He describes their lives here so affectionately despite the way Hemingway cultivates a lifestyle of relative poverty as a writer that seemingly is always relying on the odd cheque arriving for an article he had submitted. The area still retains a character today but back in the 20's it was a place far removed from the modernity and chic of Paris today. They were clearly a very happy family unit in this lively area.

Retrace your steps back towards Place Contrescarpe and look out for Rue Rollin on your left, a street that leads through to Rue Monge. This route is worth the detour for a couple of reasons. Rue Rollin makes you feel as if you are in a provincial town rather than a city like Paris. To me it almost felt like a street in Burgundy, a town like Beaune. The real surprise of Rue Rollin comes at the end as you emerge onto Rue Monge. There is an extraordinary exit. It is a cul-de-sac for cars but there are two flights of steps either side of the street and these go down a beautiful frontispiece facing the street. This is bedecked with plants and flowers and if you are here at the right time of year with everything in full bloom it is a gorgeous photo opportunity.

Once you are onto Rue Monge and if you have an interest in architecture, particularly art deco then it is worth a short walk across the road. Start heading to the right, finding the Metro station Monge. Admire the front of the Metro with the beautiful ironwork on the entrance. A great photo shot in black and white.

Go back the way you came and stay on that side of Rue Monge for a genuine unexpected surprise.

It may be that you are completely unaware that Paris has its own Roman amphitheatre, a genuine one from the first century AD. Neither did I until some years ago when we stayed at a hotel on Rue Monge – Hotel des Nations St-Germain and very pleasant it was too.

Across the street there was a sign above a passageway at No. 47 Rue Monge over which was a stone carving of a Roman soldier's helmet. The sign said 'Arenes de Lutece' but there was certainly no great fanfare accompanying it. As you watched from the window of our hotel the daytime scene of people busying themselves with the business of getting to work and school, watching the tourists making their way down to the Seine and the Islands, you hardly ever saw anyone going through the gateway.

If you go to the front of the entranceway there is a little more information (in French) as to what lies beyond. Looking down the short passageway it has to be admitted the prospects are a little unpromising. However it is definitely worth stepping inside. As you emerge into the light the area gives off the appearance of a small park, perhaps a children's play area and here you may well encounter some youngsters playing soccer. Unmistakably though you are now in a very well preserved, compact Roman Arena. It is a pleasant space, away from the traffic noise of Rue Monge. It is a place where people may sit and read or just stroll through on their way to work. It will have very few tourists so please make a visit. When you return home you can amaze your friends with this discovery and your knowledge of hidden Paris.

Time to move on with a pleasant stroll down Rue Monge and then left onto Rue des Ecoles until you come to Rue Racine on your left. The goal of this walk is to reach Polidor restaurant, certainly a Hemingway destination and this historic building was heavily featured in 'Midnight in Paris'. Even if you are not going to dine here (cash only – no cards) it is well worth a look and again bring your camera (or these days your phone). Before we get to Polidor it repays a few moments pause outside the Restaurant Bouillon Racine previously known as a Chartier Restaurant. This is a building of Art Nouveau splendour both outside and in and is in fact listed as a historical monument of Paris.

Apart from boasting a fine reputation for its food

it has another much darker claim to fame. One of the most extraordinary verdicts in a French murder trial came after an event that took place in the street outside this restaurant. On May 25th 1926 the President in exile of the Ukrainian National Republic, Symon Petliura was assassinated by a man named Sholom Schwartzbard. He claimed to have lost all 15 members of his family in Jewish pogroms in the East. This was a horror that he held Petliura personally responsible for. Schwartzbard made no attempt to flee from the scene nor did he in any way claim that he was not responsible for the murder. Despite the cold hard facts of the evidence he was acquitted by the French jury basically on the grounds that his actions were justified. In effect such a man as Petliura had no right of protection because of his alleged crimes. It is not a verdict we would expect today but it is one that had been argued previously and it has a place in French history. It is still a verdict that resonates today with the animosity between Ukraine and Russia. The prosecution at the trial put forward that Schwartzband was in fact a Russian agent and that view holds good to many Ukrainians even now.

There is plenty of interest on the streets of Paris and it always repays the effort of seeking it out.

On the left hand side as you continue along Rue Racine you come to Rue Monsieur le Prince and there is the venerable Crémerie-Restaurant Polidor.

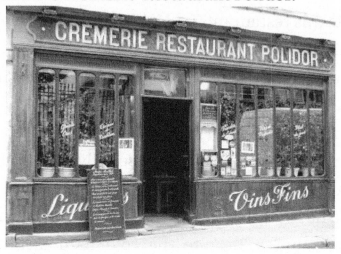

This eating place is a throwback to the times of Victor Hugo and of course Hemingway and the contemporary artists and writers. The interior is little changed from the days Hemingway would have patronised this restaurant. It plays a central role in 'Midnight in Paris' although it has to be said there is not a sign of the laundromat that Polidor transforms into.

This is a restaurant to savour with a menu that is right out of the Belle Époque and they have no intention of changing any time soon thankfully. The exterior is a remarkable throwback to another age and one of the finest photo opportunities in Paris. You may have to be more sociable than usual and share a table.

From here it is a relatively short walk to the Boulevard St Germain and on to three café/restaurants that are synonymous with the writers of Paris. Brasserie Lipp is often referred to by Hemingway in 'A Moveable Feast' and it takes little imagination today to place this establishment in its historical context. It always feels very 20's/30's to me and certainly sets the mind racing as you contemplate the stories the tables could tell. Hemingway famously goaded the 'friends' he had cruelly portrayed in his novel to come at an arranged time and shoot him at a Brasserie Lipp table. Across the road are the two famous cafés that always seem to be in competition for clientele and of course they are. They have historically competed for the favour of writers and artists down the decades. Some preferred to sip a coffee for hours and write at a table at Café de Flore and some at Le Deux Magots. Some fell in and out of favour with their regular haunt and interchanged the two.

Today it is a must see destination for many and plenty of visitors are happy to pay a coffee price that would have horrified Hemingway and others who were allowed to sit and write for a few centimes back in their day. It is undeniably an experience and just once maybe it is worth the cost to watch the world go by.

You can have that world just wondering if you may be a 'someone' which of course you are to your family and friends. It is a little game to play for a pleasant moment in time.

I have only scratched the surface of artistic Paris and the historical gems that are to be found. I do encourage you to do more research and have a clear plan before you go. There is so much to see and experience beyond the obvious. You will take so much more away with you in memories and knowledge if you dig deeper than the 'tourist' sites. It also depends on how far you wish to walk and for that reason it seems the right time to bring this chapter to a close. Be assured however that there is far more than I have portrayed waiting to be discovered.

To finalise I will take you back to the river and the Pont Neuf at the very tip of the Île de la Cité. As you go over the bridge coming to around the midway point of the island you find a narrow street on the right. Going through this entrance way the narrow road opens up into a most beautiful space – Place Dauphine. For me this is a very favourite spot in Paris, a quiet place with many relaxing cafes and restaurants intertwined between the gorgeous apartments. It is leafy and tranquil yet but a stone's throw from the noisy hordes congregating around Notre Dame. It is clear that few tourists even know this is here and selfishly long may that continue. It is a delightful space and to eat here or just enjoy a coffee is a joy. The pretty cobbled streets of Place Dauphine inevitably appeared in 'Midnight in Paris'. If you go and sip a coffee at Restaurant Paul at number 15 Place Dauphine you can if you close your eyes just hear the gentle sound of the horses hooves drawing the approaching Belle Époque carriage along to the terrace.

You can certainly imagine that scene. The ambiance of this square has retained its charm effortlessly down the decades – a place to savour and to relax.

Hemingway burned his bridges with his

'friends' in Paris, cruelly portraying many of them as characters in his novels, making no attempt to hide as to who he was basing his writing on. Most of all he discarded the woman he loved and lost the stability of the family he had around him. He has left a romantic portrait of Paris that is portrayed in 'Midnight in Paris' and like much of the best art and music this is a legacy based on the suffering of the tortured artist. His footsteps make for an interesting walk through this quarter of Paris.

I could walk farther but I am as my friends have complained perhaps a little over active in that department. So I will consider a wider audience  and end my tour sitting at the terrace of Restaurant Paul – but tomorrow is another day.

SEARCHING FOR A
HEART OF GOLD

Actually this particular search ended some time ago. We were poised to travel to Paris with the aforementioned 'Heart of Gold' June to celebrate her 40th wedding anniversary. The search, and he did not have to look far, had for her husband John reached a happy conclusion all those years ago. What though has Neil Young got to do with our travels to Paris and especially on such a special occasion that this particular year had provided? Well, quite a lot actually in 2008. Anyway I digress as usual.

On Thursday March 6th 2008 I was sitting with my son James in the Hammersmith Apollo, London some two and half hours into a remarkable set by Neil Young. I remark to James that as Young builds 'Rocking in the Free World' to an inspired frenzied climax that 'if anyone lights a match now the whole building will explode'. Anyone who was there that night will understand my emotions at witnessing this incredible performer in glorious full flow. Twenty minutes later I say to James that even though Young is launching into his classic anthem 'Like a Hurricane' at the start of his encores we really must leave. For one thing I am unsure that the car park where we left our vehicle is not due to be locked up with our car inside. For another thing I really do have to get home to Lancashire.

You see I have a train to catch at Preston station in no more than eight hours' time en-route to Paris and the above mentioned celebration. To be here in London just after midnight is not the most sensible decision I have ever made but a man's gotta do etc.... We run down the stairs with the deafening strains of Young's searing guitar chasing us out of the arena. From there we head across Hammersmith St Pauls Green, manoeuvring a dangerous traverse of Hammersmith Bridge Road to finally reach the car park which thankfully is still open although troublingly deserted. I have seen concerts at Hammersmith Apollo (or Odeon as was) many times over the years but never having travelled here by car before. The mechanics of extricating ourselves from London to head North at this hour are a daunting prospect.

I do know that not getting home in time to be on Preston station is not an option – I have to be on that train.

We head around the North Circular Road and out onto the M1 and despite a short hold up we arrive safely home at about 3.30am. My wife Niamh is extremely grateful to be woken up at that hour but I try to focus on getting a couple of hours sleep. Of course I fail miserably. A very tired and dishevelled self appears on the train station shortly afterwards feeling totally unready for more travel. At least I was there despite my crazy schedule of the previous twenty four hours.

It is not my intention to fully describe this trip as it stretched over several days but as the previous twenty four hours had been so compelling I will focus on the first twenty four hours or so in Paris as it was eventful and very memorable. Oh, and Neil Young makes a comeback.

Our hotel, a relatively modest Ibis (our merry group prefers to spend our money on wine and food) is located in the Cambronne area. This is in fact a convenient location with a Metro station right outside, quite literally really as it was at raised level over the street. It was also not far for us to walk at night in our usual quest for good restaurants. As always with an Ibis in France the hotel staff are welcoming and the rooms are spotlessly clean. In this one it has to be noticed that the bathroom is extremely small - broom cupboard small. Even I of relatively slim build have difficulty turning around in the confined space. One of the friends in our party is not of slim build and he would be the first to concede on that observation. It did cross our mind about how he would use the facilities but wisely we did not strike up a conversation on that point. He did though seem to keep up his usual high standard of grooming on the trip.

I was an extremely relieved man when by a majority decision it was decided that we should eat in the hotel restaurant tonight – I was very, very tired to say the least. The Ibis is modern and although we have dined in an Ibis before in other parts of France and been more than satisfied I felt a little guilty in voting for staying in tonight. I assumed the restaurant would be quite soulless. I could not have been more wrong. I have referred previously in my other writings to the irreverent (well certainly to the French) British sitcom 'Allo 'Allo. This dealt with basically a theme of a setting placed during the German occupation and the devious

French café owners and impossibly attractive female resistants outwitting the incompetent German officer customers at every turn. 'Leessen I vull zay zis unly vonce' – that sort of thing. Anyway as we were shown to our table this restaurant certainly took me back to that pastiche setting and times past – all red checked tablecloths and wooden bar.

What a meal we had, all rustic country fare.

Pate to start and then hearty beef bourguignon or entrecote steak with sautéed potatoes and Îles flottantes to finish. All washed down with carafes of honest country wine – absolutely perfect but totally unexpected. To say we staggered happily to bed would be downplaying the joy we found in such a corporate setting – we are in Paris and settled.

We convene in the hotel lobby after breakfast and form a plan of action for the day. My suggestion as the hiking tour coordinator is that we walk from the Arc de Triomphe to the Islands along the straight line of sight through the Tuileries Gardens. In retrospect, although for me it was a short stroll, for others it may have been a touch farther than their usual walk to the local corner store for a pint of milk. In fact our aforementioned friend could not possibly undertake such a distance.

However, he and his wife suggested that they were more than happy to bail out when they had walked sufficiently far and go on to the Islands by Metro. So with everyone agreeing on a contingency plan we headed by Metro over to the Place de l'Étoile and the starting point of our tour along the Champs-Élysées to Notre Dame. For Niamh and myself the route is very familiar and we are happy to keep up a steady pace. For most of the rest of our party the sights and sounds of this area of Paris are a new and exciting experience and they choose to linger along the way, most notably in front of jewellery and perfume stores.

It soon becomes apparent that to reach the Islands by lunch time is going to be unlikely. Progress will need some serious encouragement  from the group leader – me. Listening to my pleadings is not going to happen and the pace slows even more. Eventually we did reach the Place de la Concorde for a group photo but I notice that the said photo contained our two friends who should have headed for the Metro some time ago. Although the pace is slow he is still struggling greatly with the distance and heat of the day and has a face like thunder. I would like to ask him why he is still with us despite the discomfort and the binding agreement we had at breakfast but leave him to make up his own mind as to when to head for the transport.

We press on across the Place and in to the Jardin de Tuileries, so named because of being constructed on the site of old tile works and now a very beautiful and atmospheric feature of Paris. It is a glorious spring day and we stroll slowly by the round ponds with their fountains. Small toy boats are being floated by a few children. We carry on towards the Place du Carrousel, its monument perfectly in line with its larger twin at the top of the Champs-Élysées.

As is quite normal for me I again find this place a contradiction in emotions and feelings. On one level I just love this place and despite the gardens generally being very busy with tourists and locals it unfailingly gives off a sense of peace and calm. This is especially true when you are sat at one of the old green painted tubular seats that have featured in many a photo or artworks.

Yet here the historical side of my character gets immersed in the events that have occurred here over the years. You can mentally escape back to the times of the French revolution when the gardens contained a palace for the French Royal family. Despite attempting to escape through the gardens this beautiful space was in effect a prison for the doomed monarchy. The merciless massacre of their Swiss guards in the Tuileries is at odds with the calm today.

Historically for me the gardens are more synonymous with the fighting that occurred particularly at the end of the German occupation. I can visualise the destroyed tanks near the entrance, a sight that would seem so incongruous today. You feel at the centre of the city here and what an atmospheric open space to have, one of the finest in any capital city in the world.

I stand at the top of the steps in front of the Carousel, Eiffel tower sellers at my back trying to make me turn around, when I see that a few yards behind our party Angus is still with us. He looks very close to collapse and I just don't understand why he has not, as agreed, taken the Metro. We are now well past the point of no return and the only way is forward. I wisely move on before I have to make eye contact.

We all rest by the Louvre pyramid before heading over the Ponts des Arts and finally get to the Islands passing by the King Henry statue. At that point there was what you might call a difference of opinion. It is a fairly short one as Angus now takes himself off from the group and goes in search of sustenance. His walk is not going to end at Notre Dame. It is true to say that the rest of us feel a little guilty but console ourselves that we only did as we said we would and his dissatisfaction was really of his own making. We still love him really. To be honest we are all tired by now and decide to go in search of Angus and his wife and food and wine but not necessarily in that order. We spy them at a restaurant table at a corner of the Boulevard Saint Michel with a glass of wine in his hand and clearly waiting for instant food service – we decide to leave him be.

Walking through the Latin Quarter in search of a table I am fully aware that this is going to end badly. There is no possibility that any of these restaurants on these busy side streets are going to give satisfaction but as I said we are tired. One of our party makes the fatal mistake, one you are warned about so often, of being tempted into a restaurant by the smiling waiter at the door who points out lovely photos of the wonderful food to be supplied to the tired tourist. But we are in or rather we are captured. I suppose we could have dragged him out but no one has the energy. I know that this is going to be dreadful but we will have to make the best of it.

Anyway, the first course is French onion soup and no Frenchman could possibly make anything but a fine onion soup. Clearly the chef is not French. I assume they do not have a dishwasher in the kitchen but always reuse the washing up water for the first course. This awful watery concoction did not even come with any bread and cheese. At least it did not fill us up before the next courses. Next is beef (and I use that term advisedly) bourguignon and the least said about that the better. I had another sip of wine and placed a couple of notes on the table and said I would wait outside. I did not have to wait long as everyone slid away from the table and ran. I think we covered the bill but should really have held some money back for the inevitable visit to the chemist.

All part of life's rich travel tapestry.

Fortunately we had eaten so little of the lunch that we were expectantly ready for something much more agreeable. This was the highlight of our trip – an evening Bateaux Mouches cruise along the Seine with dinner to celebrate John and June's ruby wedding. We all met in the foyer, freshly scrubbed and most of us resplendent in new clothes. Most of all we are friends again after our rather fractious expedition down the spine of Paris that morning. For my part I had forgiven whoever was the first to inexplicably go into the lunchtime restaurant and reserve us all a table.

The Bateaux Mouches cruise leaves from a jetty that has the Eiffel Tower as a backdrop. The daylight has faded sufficiently for the lights from the tower and along the quay to be gently reflected in the river on what is a very still balmy evening. This is a new experience for all of us and despite inevitably feeling a bit touristy we are a genuinely excited party as we go up the ramp into the boat. It does have the feel of Renoir's 'Boating Party', yes it is modern and all comfort provided, but the atmosphere is warm and convivial. There is an easy relaxed manner displayed by the staff as they welcome us aboard and guide us to our table.

After a welcoming glass or two of champagne we are thoroughly content, now excited and happy, ready to play our roles in this theatre on the water. My personal expectations for the food are not high. I am assuming that catering on what must be a restricted space will be difficult and corners will inevitably be cut.

Not so.

Our first course consists of the most succulent scallops, pan fried to a golden perfection and served with a dressing of such depth and quality that you are reaching for the five star review already. The wines are fine ones, a glorious chilled crisp Chablis and reds from Burgundy. The bottles are always available and not restricted to the whim of the waiter making the decision that you need a refill.

The finest example of Dover sole follows the scallops and is cooked to perfection, basted in lemon and brown butter. Then the cheese course and a glass of fine port before the dessert course though I trust you may appreciate that I have no recollection of what that was but I do remember they insisted on a delicate Armagnac to conclude. At some point during this feast a photographer appeared to take all our individual portraits and I still have mine. I can only conclude that it was taken somewhere around the dessert course. I do vaguely remember the cabaret chanteuse who brought a mellow end to this evening of delight.

The meal was superb but the star of the evening was still Paris. To see the city from the river and at night is extraordinary and an experience to be cherished and always recalled. The highlight of the cruise had to be passing by Notre Dame, so atmospheric in the evening light that it took your breath away. It is such a gentle way to travel and spend the most unforgettable evening with dear friends. We staggered away from the gangplank very happy indeed, memories and friendships set in stone. Despite our extensive wining and dining we all agreed that this time all of us were going to walk the full distance back to the hotel. This was a night to savour, not to end. So the city was all ours and we made the most of what it still had to show us as we started up the Champs des Mars. Not though before we had all stretched out on the ground underneath the Eiffel Tower, cameras pointing to the top for that most obvious of shots but one that just had to be done. The photo of us all on the ground in a starburst circle was actually the more interesting shot.

That is our twenty four hours or so, we survived it and were conscious enough for the most part to recall the most treasured of times with the dearest of friends. It was Paris at its best, a Paris that responds to your mood and takes you to places that you do not know exists, with total satisfaction and reminiscences to come for years afterwards.

Oh sorry - Neil Young. Well we so enjoyed his London concert and this subsequent trip to Paris that we thought we might repeat it, just the two of us. Later that same summer he came back to England to play an open air concert at a venue called the Hop Farm in Kent. We went to that one with our son, stayed overnight, tossed him the car keys and we headed off to Paris on the Eurostar from Ashford. The year had gone full circle and most pleasantly and memorably so.

7TH

ARRONDISSEMENT

– Beyond Rue Cler

At the outset I have to make it clear that some of my best friends are American, as indeed are a good number of my wife Niamh's extended family – the Irish get everywhere. However it seems to me that even you adventurous American tourists are complaining about the number of your compatriots that populate Rue Cler in the 7th Arrondissement, a now famous street within sight of the Eiffel Tower. It is as so many of you point out – the Rick Steeves effect. So is it worth going to this area of Paris or is it devoid of a true Parisian experience? I have to say that I like Rue Cler even though it has something of an 'American in Paris' theme about it. If that comes across too strongly for you then be assured there is life beyond Rue Cler in this fascinating arrondissement. I hope you don't mind but this part of the book will veer towards reading a little more like a guide book but I think this area of Paris repays a little more exploration than seems to be given to it by many visitors. Anyway, dining especially is a serious business in Paris.

Like anywhere that is popular with tourists Paris will always have areas that certain groups will congregate in. Montmartre may be an area where more English tourists will find accommodation. You may find that the Japanese will gather more centrally in Paris. It has to be said that Rue Cler is most certainly an American enclave just as Lourmarin in Provence is a place they love and gather. The English in Provence will head for Menerbes, the village that Peter Mayle called home in 'A Year in Provence'.

On Rue Cler you have two cafés in particular that have become American clubs in reality – Café Du Marche and Le Central. It is true that some restaurants on Rue Cler have dumbed down their menus and are providing very standard unambitious fare, photos provided for the timid visitor. The waiter you will see is languidly placing the change on the table, his eyes looking elsewhere for another victim, daring the diners to pick up the change but also making it clear that the coins should be added to, making a larger tip before leaving. There are however places to eat even on Rue Cler that can be very satisfying and authentic.

Le Roussillon is one such establishment situated at the corner of Rue Cler and Rue Grenelle and is a bistro where we enjoyed a most enjoyable lunch with attentive service.

Where Rue Cler scores highly is that away from the congregated throngs around Café Du Marche there are so many authentic Parisian shops. Wine and cheese stores, vegetable and grocers shops, butchers and delicatessens and of course the regular street markets. You will really get much more out of this area however if you look beyond Rue Cler and these are a few places we have found and enjoyed over the years in this popular neighbourhood of Paris.

The very first time we stayed in this arrondissement the hotel we chose was located just behind Rue Cler on Rue Valadon at what is now Hotel Valadon Colors. It has been completely refurbished from the time of our stay and has changed in its character but is still rated very highly. Rue Valadon is a quiet street, a virtual cul-de-sac, so is an excellent choice for the area. When we stayed we had a room with an Eiffel Tower view so it is certainly a place to consider. Just at the top of the street around the corner is a most wonderful cheese store and even if you do not go inside you will find the shop window itself is worth a few moments of your time.

My interests in any arrondissement in Paris are always connected to food, finding a fine restaurant in Paris is one of the utmost joys in life. Also you may have gathered I have a great love of history and that is well catered for in this area. Recently we made what can be viewed as a slight mistake in visiting Paris in August, the very time that most Parisians leave Paris and that includes many waiters and restaurateurs. We were very limited in our dining choices and did not really want to eat at the popular spots on Rue Cler.

We were staying just around the corner from Rue Cler at the Hotel de la Motte Picquet and the clue to its address is in the name. This is a lovely unpretentious three star hotel that gives excellent friendly service, clean rooms and welcoming public areas with interesting views on to the lively Avenue de la Motte Picquet. It does not however have a restaurant so it is always a case of dining out for the evening. We passed the boisterous tables and bars of the upper end of Rue Cler, giving thanks that we were not eating there. There was the thought that there appeared to be little else on offer –'les vacances d'été' were in full swing and the closed signs were out in profusion.

Farther along Rue Cler we reached Rue de Grenelle and going to the left you come to number 167 where there is a small Italian restaurant called Le Den. It was open and it had three tables out in the street and on a balmy evening this seemed like an oasis in a dining dessert.

This super little restaurant also seems to double as a deli. It serves wonderful Italian food including pizza of course, food made with fresh seasonal ingredients. It was  in total contrast to the mainly conveyer belt tourist food just round the corner on Rue Cler.

We were given lovely service from the young ladies who coped smilingly as extra tables were spread out along the street to accommodate all the diners that kept on coming. You did feel a little like you were an advertisement for the restaurant as people stopped to look and admire the dishes on the tables. The raviolo especially was wonderful and I would also encourage you to try the risotto. The panna cotta was definitely the dessert to go for and the house wines are a cut above the standard you may have expected. This was a very popular place and will be more so if they get the name confusion sorted out on the awnings and shop front. I am not quite sure where Le Den comes from as a name but if you are searching for it that is the name to enter in Google. So it is a case of going early or making a reservation.

We ended up on our three night trip dining here every evening and we don't usually do that on our travels. Yes I would have to make the point that it is on a fairly busy street but it still has a great ambiance especially as the light fades and you feel that you are in an authentic Parisian neighbourhood. We found this to be a hidden gem of a restaurant in this touristy part of Paris. You can also book on Le Fork which is always a bonus.

If, unlike ourselves, you are sensible enough not to visit Paris in August when the heat is humid and sensible Parisians have abandoned the city, then you have some exceptional choices of eating venues.

There are two in particular that are the epitome of classic French restaurants, in different ways as perfect a Parisian dining experience as you will find. They are also very close to one another just a short stroll from Rue Cler across Avenue Bosquet.

The first one is the most charming (and petite) restaurant Le P'Tit Troquet at 28 Rue de l'Exposition, a quiet virtually car free cul-de-sac of a street. Think of going to someone's home for a meal, a table spread modestly but attractively and you are the special guest to be fussed over and pampered. This is Le P'Tit Troquet. On the occasion we dined there we went with two friends who trusted me that I would make a memorable choice for them and they were not disappointed.

We walked into the small dining space set out with a few tables, a scene that seemed to be out of a French movie, so intimate and welcoming. The first and obvious impression we gained was that all the tables were occupied and as I had booked in advance this was a little disconcerting. The lady in charge of front of house (and it is a very small house) came over offering us a large beaming smile of welcome and led us through the tables to an even smaller room at the back of the restaurant. This room had only four small tables which were all beautifully prepared. This was exactly like someone's dining room at home and the feeling that you were a welcomed guest was enhanced every time you had an interaction with the lady or the waiting staff – a special place indeed.

The menu is classic French cuisine, beef bourguignon served temptingly en cassolette, steak, duck, monkfish, sea bass and vegetarian options. The desserts are classics with a twist, Rum baba, chocolate mi-cuit and a Crème Brulee which does not have a twist – pure classic French. The wine is expertly chosen and complimentary to the meal. The room feels as if it is unchanged from seventy years ago. A room that could double as a film set from the war years and just after. Probably in those days totally smoke filled and each table occupied with romantically involved couples. It is a quite captivating ambiance and one exploited to the full in this intoxicating restaurant by the welcoming owners. Not to mention a chef with a repertoire steeped in the fine culinary history of France and Paris. He is a craftsman producing dishes that are firmly in context with the restaurant and the atmosphere of this super little establishment.

As we left that evening, my companions found it very difficult to find words that fully expressed the experience they had just savoured. We noticed for the first time a small galley type kitchen to the left – I do mean small. There was the chef and one assistant who incredibly produced this classic French feast in such a tiny space. He smiled as we peered inside, confident that all was well with the dishes he had sent out to our table. He was totally justified in that confidence as we bid him good night and stuttered our grateful thanks.

Classic but on a slightly different scale and setting is the popular La Fontaine de Mars just at the end of the same street at 129 Rue Sainte Dominique. This restaurant has entertained presidents and celebrities but is not in the least pretentious.

Again the classic French theme is portrayed by the red checked tablecloths and the wood panelling around the bar and inside the restaurant. It is a restaurant that in summer becomes open plan and spills tables out onto the street. The service is warm and friendly but it is very Parisian and just as you would expect in such a restaurant very rooted in its tradition.

The menu is not experimental, just straight out of the French cookery school manual. Steak of course, duck confit, coq au vin, blanquette de veau, Burgundian snails, sole meuniere, foie gras if you wish and desserts following the same tried and tested traditions. All accompanied by wine by the glass and all the traditional aperitifs and digestifs on offer. It is relatively expensive but not overwhelmingly so. If you wish the wine list does stretch to some eye watering levels and if Chateau Petrus is your desire then you will find it here at a price. On the night we dined there I had the special on the menu which was a gorgeous fresh loin of cod with a perfect aioli sauce and simply cooked turned potatoes. To follow it was that most perfect of French desserts – Iles flottantes 'Fontaines de Mars' and very fine it was.

Eating on a table outside and virtually on the street is not without its challenges though. On the night we were there the restaurant and surroundings were 'entertained' for a while by a fairly inebriated beggar who was making a nuisance of himself by going back and forth along the street hoping for a few coins to be tossed in his direction. He wasn't aggressive but a bit loud at times and lacking in tunefulness and not really helping any romantic atmosphere that some were certainly hoping for. It all ended by the loud sirens of a police van that screeched to a halt and instantly 'scooped' him up into custody. At last peace reigned but as with any city Paris sadly does have its darker side and there are many unfortunate people that do not have the luxury of dining in the way we have been able to do this evening. The whole episode was a little comedic in how it was enacted and unfolded but still left you dismayed and sad that in our society there are ones reduced to this state.

From a historical or architectural standpoint you cannot avoid the fact that this area is totally dominated by one structure and that is the large tower at the end of the Champs de Mars. Once you are at the tower and you have taken all the photos from every angle  and perhaps gone across to the Trocadero and taken the shot from the vantage point of the Palais de Chaillot, a view that I feel gives the most dramatic -aew of the tower as you look through it down to the Ecole Militaire and Les Invalides then take a moment to find some more recent history.

A pause for thought and reflection. If you go to Bir Hakeim Metro station which is to the right of the tower looking from the Trocadero you will find a monument to a tragic time in French history - a memorial that was only erected fairly recently. It is a statue to commemorate the appalling events of July 16/17 1942 – the "Vel d'Hiv" raid – the roundup of over 8000 Jews (Rafle du Vel' d'Hiv) to the Vélodrome d'Hiver that stood near to this spot. The tragedy was compounded by the fact that this crime against humanity was carried out mainly by the French police and not the Germans. This was only recently fully acknowledged to be the case and remains deeply controversial in France. In slight mitigation it was also clear that a few brave police did try to give an advance warning about the action and some also allowed a very small number to make their escape from the Vélodrome but the stain on French history remains.

I always find these places in Paris very poignant and I make no excuse to returning to this theme throughout my writings about Paris. I feel that you can only understand this amazing city by taking time to reflect on its past and the recent history of Paris in particular. Take a reflective moment to make that connection and remember these people and events.

The natural progression from here is back to the tower and to walk up the Champs de Mars to the Hotel des Invalides and Napoleon's tomb. France of course still reveres Napoleon (strangely enough he inspires a good deal of respect in England) and he possibly alongside De Gaulle is the most dominant figure in French history. Of course if you are reading this sat in the sunshine and holding a glass of Dom Perignon you may want to make a case for him as well.

And then there is Joan of Arc .... Anyway back to Napoleon. Or rather another event that Les Invalides is notoriously famous for and that is the trial of Alfred Dreyfus. This Jewish army officer was erroneously and wilfully convicted of espionage and treason – another event  that although occurring over 120 years ago has not disappeared from French consciousness.

Admittance to Les Invalides is free of charge although you have to pay extra for viewing Napoleon's tomb and the main area around that. Entering from the gardens on the Rue de Grenelle you make your way into the main courtyard.

This is the area where Alfred Dreyfus was humiliated in front of his peers by having his sword ceremonially broken. He was then dishonourably discharged from the army prior to his barbaric incarceration in exile before being ultimately exonerated and released  some years later. The British TV personality Davina McCall was featured in a 'Who Do You Think You Are' episode relating that she had a family connection to one of the men who fought and ultimately succeeded in proving his innocence. If you can find it online or procure a copy it is a fascinating insight into one of the most controversial events in relatively recent French history. In any case take a moment to visualize the scene in that parade ground and reflect on an innocent man in this standout case of deliberate miscarriage of justice.

Around the courtyard you will see lines of heavy cannon. It is quite a display and they date back over some 300 years or so. I can set you a small challenge.

Walk around the perimeter and look at each cannon and somewhere you will find that one of them has a spelling mistake in the casting. When you find it just spare

a thought for the man who cast that vast lump of iron, hoping that it just resulted in a fleeting embarrassment for him rather than him being sent into exile or worse. Unfortunately it was not too fleeting as we can still clearly see it today.

At the far end of the courtyard you will find a small church or chapel. Again up to this point it is free admission. If you go inside this building you can at the far end get a sense of how Napoleon's tomb is laid out and it gives quite a dramatic effect without actually having to go inside the tomb area itself.

When you leave Les Invalides by the same route you may wish to go to the right and then right again alongside the buildings and here you will find the Rodin museum which also includes sculptures in the garden area. This is a place that is often missed by the casual tourist but Rodin is very important to the French in art history . It is worth a look if you have any interest in French art and culture.

I always smile at the mention of Rodin because of that amusing scene in 'Midnight in Paris' where Gil argues a point about Rodin in favour of the tour guide (Carla Bruni) over the pompous Paul played by Michael Sheen.

Perhaps I can now take you back to Rue Cler via Avenue de la Motte Picquet and return to my theme of the time of the occupation of Paris. Before heading to your hotel and getting ready for a fine meal in this endlessly fascinating and rewarding arrondissement just stand and reflect in front of the Elementary School on the Rue Cler side of the road.

Pause and read (in French) the black plaque on the school wall. Like most of the schools in France some young pupils were forcibly taken from this school never to return, part of the over eleven thousand children that were taken from throughout France. There is no shame in shedding a tear and you will no doubt leave the scene as you return to your hotel with a deeper relationship and understanding of Paris.

AUGUST 1944
LIBERATION

- but Poignantly not for all

The occupation and subsequent liberation of Paris in August 1944 I find to be a fascinating and incredibly poignant period in the history of the city. When you read about this time you do however find that books on the subject do inevitably go over the same ground and actual fresh information on the subject is quite limited. You as a curious visitor though are able to build up a picture of life in that time and particularly about the events of August 1944. It is a familiar story but to find out more and to get to the real drama of that time period you need to dig a little deeper. Certainly a rewarding thing to do on a visit to Paris.

Around the city you will see scores of plaques on walls, buildings, churches, schools, in fact all over the city. Some of these, particularly on school walls as previously mentioned, are hard to comprehend, upsetting to read. They are usually commemorating a group of children that will have been pupils there before being deported on train convoys - never to return. You will find many of these in the Marais district but not exclusively. However the tragic numbers they commemorate are usually greater in the Marais. Some related plaques are vast, such as on the wall of the 'Righteous among the Nations' near the Shoah memorial. The vast majority throughout Paris commemorate a single individual who is specifically named and usually the memorial is placed at the spot where the person was killed or executed. I encourage you, no I urge you to be aware of these plaques . If you have an interest in history and the social aspect of Paris then you will be rewarded with your efforts to learn more and to understand a period that shaped the city as other times have through the ages.

It is true that many of these memorials can easily be walked past and never noticed. Once you become more aware of them and take an interest you will discover more and more and it adds to the value and enjoyment of your visit. There are some fine websites that pinpoint all the plaques in Paris and add detail to the names . If one or two really capture your attention then take a photograph and do some more research when you return home.

The writing in this chapter is really a story about one plaque that has really captured my attention from the moment I came across it. It is a truly remarkable story but it is not alone in that.

Before we get to that, let me point you to another memorial in the same area – this is on the Tuileries wall on the Place de la Concorde. The liberation of Paris will always be associated with the forces of General Leclerc who were the leading French forces racing to enter the city in August 1944. Although I do believe Hemingway claimed to be first to arrive. These men had been through a lot of hardship and toil to finally reach Paris. Many of them were returning to their home city after many years away from family and friends. There is a tragic story of one of these soldiers who rang his mother from the outskirts of Paris to say he was on his way and would see her later that day – he never arrived but was killed shortly afterwards. A good number of Leclerc's forces would die on the very day of entering Paris, so near to home and a new life. It is extremely sad to contemplate the effect their deaths would have on their families anticipating a reunion and an end to hostilities.

This plaque on the Tuileries wall is of one of the more high profile casualties, the tank commander of the 2nd DB of Leclerc's forces – Marcel Bizien. He was killed right at the end of the German resistance after having destroyed a Tiger tank at the entrance to the Tuileries. You can find photographs that sit incongruously with the scene today. Pictures of shattered tanks where now you stroll and sit in peace by the ponds, ice cream in hand. Just farther on towards the Seine and the Pont de la Concorde is the spot where my imagination was captured by a particularly extraordinary plaque. It is just down from the King Albert statue on the Cours la Reine on a retaining wall to your right as you start going down to the river and the Port de la Concorde. There are two names on the plaque but it was some words at the end of the inscription that grabbed my attention and curiosity. My knowledge of the French language was reasonable by now but I could not be sure I had translated it correctly as the statement seemed to be fanciful in the extreme. The plaque says that these two policemen, Gardiens de la paix, had been shot by the Germans at this spot.

The words after the second name read 'Blesse a survecu' – He survived!

Yes, there was no mistake, the plaque said that although the first man Maurice Guinoiseaux (aged 36) had been killed the other policeman Armand Bacquer, a 24 year old, had survived.

What was his story?

It is early morning on Saturday August 19th 1944 when Armand Bacquer kisses his wife Jeanne goodbye. He leaves for a meeting with other police colleagues by the twin spired Basilica Saint-Clotilde close to the Esplanade des Invalides. The police have been on strike in protest at the continuing German control of the police. The meeting is to arrange more direct action in support of what will become a more general uprising prior to liberation. The instructions at this meeting are for them all to go to the Prefecture of

Police close to Notre Dame . There they are to forcibly take control of the building from colleagues who are continuing to carry out orders from the occupying forces.

Armand along with the other policemen separate and take different routes to try to avoid attention. He goes onto the Rue de Grenelle where he observes two men attaching a poster to a wall, a poster that gives notice of a general uprising to begin in Paris. This is something in fact that the Allies who have by now decided to liberate Paris are desirous of avoiding due to the risks to the fabric of the city itself. Armand approaches the poster but is startled from behind by a command from a German soldier. He is threatening and holds his Luger pistol to Armand's neck. Armand is arrested and ultimately transferred to the Hotel Williams in Square Montholon, a building commandeered by the Feldgendarmerie. This hotel is still there today under the same name in the 9th Arrondissement just off Rue Lafayette.

The building is in chaos with the Germans under great stress and agitation. They are aware of the news that the police have turned against them and most are ready to get out of Paris and save their skins. They are highly volatile. Armand is roughly treated and verbally abused. He is also left in no doubt that he will be shot. Any thoughts of the police as complicit comrades are gone and only hatred and anger remain. In another cell in the building lies the other man on the plaque - Maurice Guinoiseaux . He was unluckily the only one arrested by a German patrol on the Rue de Rivoli from a van full of policemen taking weapons to the Cite. Just before midnight the two men are taken from the hotel and bundled into a car that stops abruptly on the Cours la Reine close to the statue of King Albert of Belgium. The two are dragged from the car and they are forced with hands in the air to the retaining wall leading to the wharf. The brutality of the moment is captured for you as you stand by the present day plaque. You realise that the Germans had deliberately arranged the execution so that the last view for the pair would be of the Seine and the Eiffel Tower – the symbol of Paris.

Later Armand would recall that in fact his last view was the face of his wife Jeanne and his father and mother on the market in Glomel, Brittany.

The weapons are

slammed shut and readied. A raking fire sweeps over the two men. It sprays from Armands legs and across his body but avoids his head as it passes to that height. As it reaches Guinoiseaux he is killed instantly. The soldier in charge shouts 'Fertig!' (finished) and they leave the scene. Armand is critically wounded but still alive.

He can hear the sirens of fire engines on the streets of Paris and in his delirium imagines they are coming to save him. His thoughts swing to fearing that the Germans are returning to finish him off. He assists his survival by sipping drops of rainwater but all the time on this wet night the river is rising and he fears that he will be drowned anyway.

It is eight hours later and the city is waking to a new day towards liberation and incredibly Armand Bacquer is still alive and able to make sounds to try to attract attention. It is eventually a passing priest that hears him. The comfort he initially gives confuses Armand and he fears he will die. The next thing he is aware of is a fireman's helmet and it is only then that he realises he has a chance of survival. The Germans are not going to return, he is comparatively safe now. He has been shot fourteen times but astonishingly each bullet has missed a vital organ. The wall behind will testify that the bullets have mainly passed through his body.

His ordeal is not over and he will hover between life and death for several weeks in the Necker Hospital where he was operated on by a Professor Huet.

He eventually makes such a fine recovery that he returns to his role as a policeman at the station in the Rue De Bourgogne. This is close to the original meeting at the Basilica and just over the river from where he was shot. His colleagues appropriately give him the name 'Living –Death' but he lives to retire in 1975 before dying peacefully in bed in the early part of the new millennium. On the 19th August 1994 he was made a Commander of the Legion of Honour by President Mitterand on the 50th anniversary of the Liberation of Paris.

This is just one of the remarkable stories behind the plaques of Paris. Please take a moment to discover more about some of the fascinating history of this great city and the men and women who formed the shape of the Paris we have to enjoy today. His late son Joel Bacquer kept this story very much alive and I am indebted for some details from his writing of the events. Other accounts are available on the internet, usually in French.

OUT ON THE
STREETS OF PARIS

– A cautionary tale

I have always

found the streets of Paris to be extraordinarily safe. I feel far more secure to be walking through them at night than in my infinitely smaller hometown. In fact there is no way I would be walking home on the streets of Blackburn in the dark or come to think of it at most other times thank you very much. However there have been some occasions in Paris where we have had to have our wits about us. Minor ones of course are found with the numerous scams that are operated on the streets and particularly in the more touristy areas. It always amazes me how people still fall for such nonsense as the 'ring scam' but sadly they do.

More seriously we have had two encounters that I would rather have avoided. One was my own fault in going into a dubious area in the first place and the other was unavoidable but fortunately obvious to us so there was some advance warning.

That one was at Abbesses Metro station on the western side of Montmartre. Now I am sorry but Montmartre as of yet is not my favourite area of Paris. I know for many Montmartre IS Paris and they love it but I have never really got on with it. I find part of the area around Sacre Coeur reminds me of an open toilet with some vile aromas and I just find some of it a bit fake with so many trying to extract a few Euros from the tourists at every turn. It is a place I should love really as it is synonymous with many of the Impressionist painters I love but I haven't managed it as yet – I really must try harder. I think I need to find a hotel here and immerse myself in the real Montmartre. Set me down on the bridge between the two Islands on the Seine or in the Place Dauphine and I am a very happy man. I concede that Montmartre is a photographer's dream and I do appreciate that aspect of it but it is not an area I rush back to. Sorry, but don't give up on me yet.

At the Metro station we were awaiting the next

train, the sound filtering down the distant tunnel, when I became aware on the platform of a fidgety young man just to my right. After a minute or so it became very obvious that he had me in his sights as he shadowed every move I made. I was certain he was going to make a play for my camera bag. I told my son that when the train comes in we should take different doors and he should come round inside the carriage to meet me as I get on. This was what we planned.

The Metro train came into the platform and sure enough the young man cut deliberately in front of me as he stepped onto the train. As he did so he 'stumbled' and a selection of cards fell from a wallet he was holding onto the floor by the open doors of the train. The natural reaction is to help to pick them up but I was convinced this was a ruse to get me to the floor. As he bent down, expecting me to do the same, he grabbed my camera bag and tried to pull it away from me.

I am not sure what possessed me then but in retrospect it was a little stupid in view of what might have been the consequence. I lashed out at him with my foot and landed a substantial blow. He reeled back, got up and ran off the train and down the platform before rushing up the stairs and out of sight into the street.

He did not get the bag and the fake cards were still strewn over the carriage floor. Then bizarrely, and I have to say embarrassingly, the occupants of the carriage burst into a loud round of applause for my actions. I certainly wasn't a hero. As I said, in retrospect it was not really a sensible thing to have done but it was just an instant reaction. Fortunately as he had bent down it made it possible that for once I was facing someone who for that moment was smaller than me – that does not happen very often.

The one other time I did not feel at all comfortable on the Paris streets was when we made an unnecessary shopping trip. The girls in the party wanted to visit the famous Tati department store, a store founded at the end of the last war and notable for its incredibly low prices and eclectic selection of goods. I gave in to their pressure and off we went.

The nearest Metro station is Barbes Rochechouart and this is in the 18th Arrondissement just north of the Gare Du Nord. That in itself should have set alarm bells ringing. On emerging from the Metro we encountered what I can only describe as a scene that could have been set in the middle of a West African market. This performance extended to the escalators leading up to the street. All types of goods from these warmer climes were on offer. I am pretty certain a live chicken would have been despatched and shoved into a bag for your supper should you so desire.

Going up the escalator it was really a case of running the gauntlet as every possible kind – and I do mean every possible kind - of services were offered. The voodoo experience and tarot card readings were definitely a bit freaky but it was the menacing air of implied violence that really got to us.

We emerged at the top into a maelstrom of activity, none of which we wanted to be a part of. The saving grace was that we could clearly see the Tati store just to the right and I pushed everyone through this throng of menacing humanity and into the store.

How to describe Tati – difficult. It is unlike any other store I have ever been in. Let's think. Hopefully you are familiar with the range of Primark stores, not that I have ever been in one but people have told me about them. Imagine someone has taken over a Primark store and slashed all the prices ruthlessly, to the extent that whoever made the goods must be paying them for the privilege – go on, that's not too hard to imagine. Then imagine that they had done away with any frills about displaying the goods and just thrown them into piles of random merchandise.

All you can see are hundreds of heads buried in the goods and rummaging through for a bargain. I think I was on the verge of passing out as I can just about cope with shopping as long as it is in quiet, perfectly presented independent stores. This was a culture shock that was way beyond my comprehension. I gave everyone a few minutes to make a purchase and then hustled them all outside.

"For goodness sake don't turn left" was my command.

We walked speedily back towards civilization as we know it, without a backwards glance.

I appreciate there are many intrepid travellers out there that risk life and limb for that unique travel experience and you are probably one of them but that was for me the scariest experience I have ever had – what a wimp!

LE REMINET AND
USING YOUR FORK

A friend of mine at my former place of pension gathering employment always cut out offer vouchers from newspapers or any source really. She meticulously searched online for internet offers and never ever paid full price for any purchase. In fact I think she got paid to take things off their hands sometimes.

I always had an aversion to doing that, just a bit embarrassed to hand over a voucher in front of staring eyes or probably I am just a snob really. I think my mind set changed when I acquired a needy and persuasive granddaughter. Suddenly bargains were required to keep up the economic pace. This recollection neatly brings me back to Paris and to my current writings about the city in this book.

About five years ago we happened to be in Paris on a short visit and I got a text message from my good friend John from over in California. He suggested that a location on the Left Bank should be a considered venue for a fine meal. I checked the restaurant out as you do and Le Reminet on Rue des Grands Degrés 75005 did indeed look every bit as tempting as John suggested. What was not quite so tempting was the rather pricey menu - John gets a better exchange rate than I do as a poor relation Englishman.

It was then that I discovered Le Fork, a website that gives vouchers or money off at a large range of restaurants when you reserve your table through them. I have to say it all sounded too good to be true. This was not my usual style of making a booking but Niamh and I both fancied eating at the restaurant so the internet booking was made. Reserving through the website is very easy to do and confirmation came through immediately. In fact, for a visitor it is a lot simpler than ringing up the restaurant especially if your French is a little below par.

This small and charming Left Bank restaurant is located on a pleasant side street on the opposite bank from Notre Dame. This is a quiet and amiable spot away from any crowds.

Le Reminet is tempting, a classic Parisian restaurant, all crisp tablecloths hosting fine cutlery and glasses. It comes with a homely welcoming feel - and in the  corner a classic French bar, an abundance of chalkboard menus for food and drink. The food we were served at lunchtime was of high quality and we ordered sea bass. These were not the tiny thin fillets we get in England but thick steak size fish that were probably fished in English waters. The flesh was firm and white, very succulent and a fresh catch of the day. Dessert was the finest example of French patisserie art and accompanied by a gorgeous crisp Loire Valley white, a digestif to finish, it was all an enticingly memorable experience. The one mistake we made was not to order a starter or some nibbles as everything here is cooked fresh to order and it was around thirty minutes before the food arrived. Wine on an empty stomach is not an ideal scenario. I had mentally calculated from the displayed menu what the going rate for this feast should have been but I knew that I would at least have some discount off the main course.

I was of course quite sceptical about the size of the final bill but when the waiter returned it was clear that not only had they honoured the Le Fork discount but unexpectedly had gone the extra mile with the offer. We ended up paying a sum that felt like we had been stealing from the kitchen.

So I am recommending that you book your next restaurant via Le Fork when you are in Paris. You may not be as fortunate as we were but do please give it a go. And anyway even if you do not get a discounted booking the restaurant of Le Reminet is a definite must so please seek out this super little restaurant. I feel like I should write a full length restaurant guide to dining in Paris but that would take away so much of the pleasure you gain when visiting the city and finding such agreeable places as Le Reminet. I listened to a friend and that is always good advice.

BATACLAN – CHANGING TIMES

A t around 9.45 in the evening of November 13th 2015 I received a disturbing message on my iPhone. It was from my son compelling me to turn on the TV news. Horrendous pictures were already coming in amidst all the confusion surrounding the information emerging from the streets of Paris. Unable or unwilling to comprehend the enormity of the horror before me I rang my son. He tried to explain what was unfolding in a city we both loved so much. The attacks that night by the so-called Islamic State brought an end to our innocent view of Paris. It would make it challenging to see our joyous memories gained over twenty years in exactly the same light. Our one selfish consolation surrounding our own thoughts about this magnificent city was that we had seen and immersed ourselves in it before this evil act. We had loved it so much and it had repaid us so very many times as no other place in the world could do.

Over the tragically difficult coming weeks for the people of Paris it became apparent however that Paris would recover. This was an appalling act of savagery. Yet Paris was a city that had acts of terror far surpassing this enacted on its streets over the centuries. Going back only as far as the occupation by the Nazis during World War II the population suffered far more than this awful night. Excessively more people were murdered and yet in time it recovered to be the place we had grown so fond of. Terror and uprising on a great scale occurred of course between that time of occupation and the French Revolution. Those types of events became an unwelcome but periodic sight to the Parisian population.

Arguably no other city on earth has such volatility among its people and rulers and yet somehow it is still viewed as the city for romantics, synonymous with a character that exudes joy and good times. It is a paradox, but it is essentially the reason why its ambiance and history draws you back time and time again.

I love history and I have a particular fascination with Parisian life that played out during the occupation years of World War II. Even though I qualify as a wearer of one of the cloth triangles that denoted how you were marked for eventual deportation and a likely doomed fate I somehow manage to absorb that time period with a degree of detachment. Doing so however, with a feeling of deep compassion for the people of those times and what they went through. I suppose I am able to take an historians view on events but that does not lessen the revulsion at the distressing actions of those years.

The happenings at the Bataclan theatre and other places around Paris that November night were somehow to me quite different. This was not history – it was happening right in front of my eyes albeit on a TV screen. It hurt personally to see places being desecrated by the actions of these evil men – places that were as familiar as my own street and unquestionably loved even more.

All these shocking events and the aftermath left

two questions on my mind constantly, almost burning into my thoughts:

Can we ever go back again?

Would Paris be the same?

The first of these took some resolution as parallel events in London also caused us and many others to question their normal travel plans. It would be the spring of 2017 before we would set foot in Paris again. Even then it would be after much soul searching as other incidents seemed to conspire to prevent us from doing so. Our travels for pleasure in the intervening two years were all taken in England – 'staycations' as this new form of holiday came to be known.

In 2017 our very good friends John and Elizabeth were coming to France from their home in California and we did so want to see them. Their week-long stay in Paris that spring week in May gave us the opportunity.

Would my wife Niamh want to go, indeed could she find the courage to do so as these episodes were still very raw? I hoped so, because I had already booked the trip without consulting or telling her. I thought I could persuade her to go even though in reality I had not really convinced myself that I could go through with it. There were many days when I pushed the thought to one side. I resigned myself to losing the money and just not going or even raising the subject with Niamh at all. However after talking it over we decided to go, we would not let ourselves be beaten by this devilish ideology. We would go back to the city we loved so much, one that had played a major role in our travel memories and education.

If only life were that simple.

Shortly before the time we were due to travel another terrorist attack occurred in London as six people were murdered in and around the Houses of Parliament. We would be spending extra time on our planned trip in London after the Paris leg of the journey and this new dreadful event once again cast a long shadow over our plans to travel to Paris.

Sadly, after giving it some thought we decided against making the journey. Statistically you know the odds of personally being involved in another such occurrence are small but mentally it is tough to get your head around that statistic. Reluctantly, just two days before travelling we informed John and Elizabeth that we felt uncomfortable about making the journey and of course they understood despite being very disappointed.

Then on the night before we were due to go Niamh said:

"You really want to go don't you?" and even though I knew this was a question that was putting her under pressure I said -

"Yes, I really do".

"Let's go then" she said and we set about throwing some clothes into a suitcase and organizing a taxi for the next morning. Soon before we had any more time to change our minds again we were at Preston train station and then heading south. I did not tell John.

On boarding the Eurostar for Paris at St Pancras the display screens showed the destination of Paris Gare du Nord and the date and time. I took a photo on my iPhone and messaged it to John with the words:

"Bonjour, Don't ask me how but we are on our way – see you soon".

I assume he thought us very indecisive. We also had not told our family and I thought I might save that message for later.

It gave a very strange emotion to be travelling on that train; the mood around us was unlike any other previous visits we had made to Paris. This felt like an expedition into the unknown, an unspoken danger lurked everywhere including on this Eurostar train. The world for us and our fellow travellers had changed, you could no longer take anything for granted. A pleasure trip for us had become an opportunity for warped and evil minds and you could not totally block that thought out.

But, how would we find Paris on this trip?

How had the people coped with what they had gone through?

Was Paris still a city to dream about?

We would soon find out and these are our thoughts and observations from the experience, one I thought we would never have again.

It would be fair to say that my mind set as we emerged into the drizzle of the dark night from the Gare du Nord onto the Rue de Dunkerque was one of increasing paranoia. For once it wasn't the thieves and scam artists that frequent the area outside the Gare du Nord that troubled me. It was that unseen danger, the thought that in this wonderful, beautiful city there were people that wanted to do harm – to ME. Strangely this had never bothered me at all when I had returned so many times to London, mainly on business. Especially I recalled one visit very shortly after the July

7th bombings. Paris had never held any terrors; you did not expect that of Paris - it did not make sense. We crossed over the large open area in front of the train station and found our bus stop on Rue de Saint-Quentin to wait for the number 38 bus that would take us to our hotel near the Luxembourg Gardens. Seated inside the bus stop was an African guy carrying a large, bulging bag.

His manner exuded an unsettling air about him. An elderly lady shuffled into the shelter and sat silently beside him, apparently unconcerned about his potential to do harm. My paranoia moved me to the outside. We stood by a café window that offered us a good view down the street so as to observe any approaching bus.

The electronic sign on the bus stop showed there was another nine minutes to our departure and that seemed a very long time in the distance.

I felt uncomfortable to say the least and at that moment I regretted making this journey.

Other 'undesirables' passed by in front of us and as darkness had fallen and heavier rain came down it was a very unsettling place to be hanging around. The number 38 bus turned the corner and even then my torture was not over. The vehicle became entangled in the solid traffic fighting for space on the street and took what felt like forever to reach the bus stop. Finally we were on and the African guy who to me was guilty as charged stayed in the shelter. He was only innocently after some place to shelter from the rain.

The bus was crowded and the windows steamed up, full of condensation from the damp bodies drying out in the warm Paris night. The obscured view through the glass made it difficult to know your exact position on the route to the crossing of the Seine.

At one of the next stops two rather rotund ladies of African descent staggered, well fell onto the bus. They were carrying excessively large bags containing foodstuffs and I made that observation cautiously. These two ladies were perspiring profusely from their efforts in hauling these huge bags from their source in the humid conditions of the evening.

It was only a few seconds after their arrival onto the bus and securing themselves by the middle double doors that you became aware of the most putrid smell imaginable. It permeated the entire bus and passengers were looking around trying to pinpoint the source. It was not difficult to establish – it was the bulging bags of these two colourfully attired ladies. The fish that was packed into these containers had been very dead for some considerable time and probably it had also been left to partially dry in the sun earlier in the day. It was rancid and I say that with some degree of understatement.

There is a thought that it is illegal to take Epoisses de Bourgogne cheese on to the Paris Metro but I have eaten Epoisses and I can tell you that it does not come close to getting on the scale of pungency that the contents of these bags have to be measured by.

With the greatest of relief to all in attendance the ladies gathered all their strength and hauled their consignment from the bus as it reached Chatelet, a distance of thankfully just two stops. One or two passengers begged the driver to keep the doors open but sadly even the French have succumbed to a degree to health and safety requirements. He refused as he pushed his own side window fully open. The acrid smell hung in the dense air for the rest of the journey but at least the source had gone and could add to the atmosphere no longer.

At least this incident took my mind off trying to work out the reason why each individual was on the bus. My paranoia was replaced by an overwhelming desire to control my stomach and its contents. We got off the bus early just beyond the Saint Michel stop – we could take no more of the unbreathable air on that bus. We walked in the fresh evening air along the Boulevard Saint-Michel and past Le Jardin du Luxembourg to the Hôtel Observatoire Luxembourg - our home for the next four nights. I dived inside avoiding and out of reach of anyone that meant me harm.

The fraught bus journey had added to my insecurities but we were here in familiar territory, we had made it and now I must explore and change my state of mind. I must think of the city, my beloved Paris. I need to find out how she has coped and what she is like after all she has gone through. Yes I must and I will.

Before we left England I had bought Niamh a L'Occitane travel set that featured an impressionistic Eiffel Tower view of Paris. Taking a photo of it resting on the window sill of our hotel room with a backdrop view of typically Parisian buildings overlooking a leafy square, I then sent it to our daughter asking her to guess where we were. She thought maybe London as she assumed we might have compromised and just made a short trip with the existing train tickets. She knew we had booked to see the exhibition of Princess Diana's dresses at Kensington Palace. She was astonished and maybe a touch concerned that we had ended up in Paris after all our deliberations. But she was also delighted that we had overcome our fears and uncertainty and gone back to a city that she knew we loved so much. I still have the photo, it is a reminder that we had arrived and would now do as we always did in Paris – explore and enjoy and let the city charm us once again.

The welcome here at the hotel is very warm and the staff come across to us as being very grateful that we and the other travellers have come to Paris. Tourism has suffered greatly since the events of 2015 and generally most hotels and restaurants have been under occupied.

After a good night's sleep we will head out today into familiar parts of Paris and find out how it has changed and if we can have the same feeling about our favourite city. Walking from the hotel alongside Le Jardin du Luxembourg we pass barely a soul. It is extremely quiet even taking into account that we are up and about at an early hour.

We arrive at Le Odeon and stroll just off the square to Rue Monsieur le Prince so as to take some photos of Crémerie-Restaurant Polidor, one of the oldest and most atmospheric eateries in Paris. This is a place still very much set in the past with checked tablecloths and have still maintained the policy of cash only accepted at the presentation of the bill. This institution is also famous now for its starring role in Woody Allen's film 'Midnight in Paris'. It is an extraordinary survivor in what appears to be its very original state. It cries out for some black and white photography and I am happy to oblige.

I have a feeling our time on this visit to Paris will be somewhat 'Midnight in Paris' themed, familiarity seems to be the key to getting back our fragile confidence in travelling to the city. My sense of excitement at the photographic possibilities to be enjoyed here in Paris is being rekindled.

As we head onwards to Rue St Andre Des Arts and find the covered passageway on Rue de l'Ancienne Comédie I take some photos of Le Procope restaurant. This establishment founded in 1686 claims to be the oldest of its type in France. This is a restaurant where if walls could talk they would fill volumes with the gossip and intrigues that have occurred around the tables of this grand old eatery. Looking back down beyond the restaurant and to the covered old passageway it really is a Parisian film set but all perfectly real, vibrant and atmospheric.

Just higher up from La Procope is the most

wonderful chocolate shop and other fine food stores and cafes. This is a place to linger, one for the senses and imagination.

Yes, familiar sights are to be the key to the enjoyment of this visit, the reacquainting ourselves with an old friend that has gone through difficult times. For us there is one square in Paris that always welcomes us. For me it is the finest of all and not the largest or grandest but one that screams character and that indefinable essence of the city – Place Dauphine.

This small, almost hidden space is at the western end of the Île de la Cité, a square that goes back to 1607 and Henry IV. It is also of course another location featured in 'Midnight in Paris'. It is worth walking to the end of the right hand side roadway and looking back up the street to imagine the horse drawn carriage making its way down towards the pavement café. Very atmospheric. There is something about this square that is indefinable. As you sit in the centre and let your eye wander through the shady trees around the triangular shape of the square, taking in the café tables and the restaurants that lead down both sides of the place, you feel perhaps more than anywhere else that you are in somewhere very special. Looking back to the entrance to the square you can just catch a glimpse of the city beyond. Despite being on the island that is home to Notre Dame you have a peace that could not be imagined possible in one of the most densely populated tourist spots in the world. It is a magical place in Paris. For us on this visit to the city it is also somewhere that is timeless and helps us to appreciate that no evil ideology can destroy all that we love about being here. It is restful and comforting to sit here and we start to feel so glad that we made this trip back to Paris.

The natural route from here is to head to the Île Saint-Louis which is perhaps our most favourite spot in Paris. We do that by heading to the right bank of the Island and walking past the Conciergerie, a building that I have still not been inside despite my interest in the history of this former prison of Marie Antoinette.

We walk for a few minutes around the flower and bird market en-route to the square in front of Notre Dame. We do not linger long but explore the side streets leading across to our goal of the smaller island and as always find these streets fascinating to wander through. A photo or two of the café Au Vieux Paris d'Arcole on Rue Chanoinesse with its beautiful exterior of foliage and flowers and lavender coloured tables is obligatory.

We are also rewarded with an unexpected photo opportunity as a 2CV threads its way down a narrow side street from the river – it could only be Paris.

The atmosphere is enhanced still further on the bridge connecting the two islands as we stop to listen to a quartet of musicians playing soft jazz on the bridge. The accordion player of course tunefully dominates this ubiquitous Parisian scene. We may have had our doubts over the previous weeks about coming back to Paris but they are slowly but very surely being dispelled. We embrace once again everything that we love about this wonderful city and the atmosphere it so effortlessly creates as you walk its streets and bridges. This bridge is an absolute favourite of ours. You generally will have music within earshot that  can only be produced in Paris. You have such generous views back to the rear of Notre Dame Cathedral and the small park adjacent to it. Then a panorama stretching both ways down the river with tourist boats passing regularly under the bridge. The architecture and metal balconies of the apartment buildings on both sides of the bridge shout out their location – it is all very Parisian. Then as you turn away from the musicians and carry on over the bridge you are at the Quai de Bourbon gateway to the island and the choice is yours – Berthillon ice cream or La Brasserie de l'Isle Saint-Louis with its sun lit pavement tables being attended to by traditionally attired waiters.

However for us there can be only one lunch

spot on the Île Saint-Louis and that is just around the corner at the restaurant Café Med. On our travels around France and here in Paris we have been fortunate enough to find cafes and restaurants that draw you back time and again and it is not on the basis that they have a Michelin star or two or three.

As you will already be aware, Café Med is at the top of the list as regards a place that gives far more to you than it takes from your credit card at the end of the meal. Warm and efficient service from elegant Madam, the energetic owner with her shock of blonde hair, and a young assistant well versed in how to handle the steady and regular clientele. Then there is the food which is always consistent. The selection of set three course meals is offered at varied prices, all of which astonish you at their value, seemingly impossibly cheap in such a prestigious location. It is also a café that caters for locals, for this island has a thriving resident population. It is not unusual to be seated next to a table hosting an elderly well-dressed lady who had popped out for lunch from her elegant island apartment. It is authentic – it is exactly what you want to find in Paris. There is quality house wine by the carafe as well – what more can you ask.

We enjoy Rue Saint-Louis en l'Île as we always

do, a street that has many lovely restaurants and cafes, some fine shops that are not all just aimed at the many tourists. It also has a butchers and cheese shop, enough produce on a busy street in the heart of the city that make you wish you were self-catering on your stay in Paris.

For me it is the most enjoyable street in the city and I am always reluctant to leave it. Sticking with familiarity on this visit is working extremely well for us as we ease into our stay and continuing that theme we head back across the river to the right bank and the historic square in front of the Hotel de Ville. This is a square that has played such a large part in the history of Paris and none more so than when De Gaulle returned to the city immediately after the occupation.

You have already had many of my thoughts about the history of Paris and Niamh is anxious to get to the Tuileries Gardens, a Parisian space that is her favourite and most comforting part of Paris.

To do that we have to go through grounds of the Louvre and into the place that contains the glass pyramid, a structure you can only love or hate. It is quite a view as you enter the place and look beyond the pyramid to the Carousel and beyond, a view that stretches with arrow straight precision right up to the

Arc de Triomphe that surveys the Champs-Élysées.

The Louvre museum entrance is getting busier now in the early afternoon but it is noticeable that there are far fewer Japanese and American tourists in Paris. In fact, unusually the main voices you can hear are French speakers, clearly the after effects of the terrorist attacks are still having an impact on overseas tourist numbers.

As we make our way through the Carousel the sky suddenly brightens and a shaft of light spreads down the centre walk of the Tuileries and glistens on the large ponds along the way. Looking down towards the Place de la Concorde I count barely thirty people walking this popular spot, indicative of the reduced numbers of tourists in many parts of Paris. It is a quiet gentle stroll today and even the 'Eiffel Tower' and water sellers are giving up and packing their touristy wares away and heading home. In some ways it is pleasant to have this area virtually to yourself and we can sit in almost complete solitude on the green metal chairs gathered around the fountains. This we accept is not Paris as we know it and the atmosphere has changed. Starved of the usual bustling excitement of the gardens, I wander down one of the walkways leading from the main wide path to take a few photos. I manage to take a view looking back towards the fountain and to my surprise there is no one in the shot. I suppose in some ways that makes the photo quite timeless but to be able to achieve that in mid-afternoon in late spring reflects just how quiet Paris is some 18 months after the terrorist attacks. Please come back everybody is my overriding desire – Paris needs people, it needs life and vitality, today it is bordering on a deserted theme park. Great for a photographer but I would rather see people enjoying themselves and creating that buzz and excitement so redolent of this great city.

I return to where Niamh is dozing in the chair around the fountain and so quiet is it that she is soon aware of my approaching footsteps and is ready to resume our walking tour.

Heading out of the gardens and over to the Left Bank we pass not a soul but are soon back in the bustling area of St Germain and standing outside the two famous cafés of Les Deux Magots and Café de Flore.

I am probably fairly correct in thinking that not many people who come to Paris have actually read in any great detail the works of Jean Paul Sarte and the many writers and intellectuals who frequented and worked at the tables of these two Paris institutions. However the cafés convey a Paris that exists in the imagination of most visitors and there are always plenty of customers willing to pay the prices to experience a glimpse of a unique period of time in artistic Paris.

Today we are two of them.

I have to say that I am not generally one for doing the obvious in regards to touristy experiences but I have always wanted to have the pavement café experience. As there is a table free on the terrace at Café de Flore then what better setting to do so. It is also I suppose a subconsciously way of reconnecting with Paris as it used to be, taking us back to visits here that were totally carefree and not with the subplot of real or imagined danger from the evils of terrorism.

The venerable Café de Flore does not disappoint, certainly not on price but more importantly with its timeless ambiance. Yes, I totally accept it is a touristy thing to do but it has an authenticity about it that is no doubt stage managed to a degree but they do it very well and I am seduced by it. The food menu is short but the drinks menu is long and presented to us by the ubiquitously smartly dressed waiter in the form of a small book.

We only want to sit in the sunshine with a drink and it has to be pink champagne. It is enjoyable to take the chance to sit here for as long as we wish and watch the people at the other tables and the world passing by. Forget your preconceptions of looking like a sad tourist just doing the sights, it is an experience you will remember. Admittedly an expensive one but worth every penny (or cent).

The champagne arrives and the elegant glasses are carefully placed on the table with a few nibbles on the side to go with the drinks. At the next table an exquisitely dressed and immaculately coiffured lady of a certain age was already seated having recently arrived at the café. Her small accessorised dog is sitting on her lap as is usual with a lady on her own at a Paris café. For her the service is stepped up a gear as the waiter comes over with a bottle of expensive champagne and ice bucket and he is accompanied by the manager of Café de Flore.

She is obviously a long standing client and the two men fuss and fawn over her in a very extravagant manner – the word obsequious springs to mind. She demurred about offering them a glass but they make sure she is comfortably settled at the table before finally moving away to attend to their other clients. I would gather that she has spent far more than we have over many years at the café but although her service has been choreographed a little more than ours I have to say we also have been made to feel quite special by the waiters. This is despite having spent what to us is more than we would normally do on a glass of wine but certainly not an exceptional amount for this café.

As you sit here watching the world go by you do feel a little smug and self- important as people scan the terrace tables as they pass by clearly wondering if you are 'somebody'. Well I am glad to say we are not - other than to our friends and family but it is a pleasant experience to be 'on show' if only for an hour or so. A simple pleasure, yes quite expensive, but as we still recall it fondly after a couple of years it was money well spent on a 'gift that keeps on giving'.

We decide it is time to take our leave and return to our normal simple life as peasants and with a cheery wave from our friendly waiter we head over to the Jardin du Luxembourg. The gardens are not particularly busy today with just a few people dotted about this beautiful space, a couple of children are sailing a colourful boat on the lake. I take a few photographs and then wander over to the Médicis Fountain to catch the light shining through the trees onto the water leading to the fountain – it is a superb light today.

I frame a shot but see that sadly there is a large and very dead bird on the water and prominent in the frame. I reset the shot to avoid it being in the photo but hope that one of the attendants passes by soon before any child  comes across. Back at the lake we sit for a while and enjoy the imposing architecture of the Senat and the views over the landscaped gardens.

I divert my mind from the peace of this tranquil spot and visualize the tanks taking aim at the tower above the clock to end the resistance of German snipers as the occupation came to its finale. I must stop this or at least refrain from giving Niamh a history lesson. It is a short walk from the entrance at the top end of the gardens to get back to our hotel. That has been a very enjoyable day and my rampant paranoia is toned down now to be very low on the scale of things to worry about. Paris is working its charm and hopefully we are contributing to the city repairing the damage of the terrorist attacks. There is a way to go but the signs are good.

The hotel has a restaurant attached and rather than go out into the Paris night we feel happier to stay in and eat here. Perhaps we are still not completely in the comfort zone back in our most favourite of cities. The Brasserie Le Luca connected to the restaurant is very much the standard Parisian brasserie. It happily has the feel of being a separate entity from the hotel and exists as a restaurant in its own right. The service is friendly and the room is populated mainly by locals rather than other tourists staying in the hotel. The staff will provide breakfast for the hotel guests in the morning and that will be done extremely well with plenty of freshly prepared choices and thoughtful, efficient service. Tonight we are in brasserie mood and happy to be dining in a casual manner, tired enough to allow ourselves the occasional glance at the TV above the bar that is showing the news from around France rather than the usual sporting fare; an indication that Parisian's still have weightier concerns on their minds. The food is of a good standard for such a modest restaurant and they also have an excellent wine list. From this we allow ourselves to be tempted by a fine bottle of Sancerre which always for us is synonymous with sitting at a restaurant table in Paris. The service is unfussy with the waiter always ready to pass a few words in gentle conversation. People wander in to sit at a table for maybe one course and then drift away into the night and the bar is populated by a few drinkers quietly whiling away an hour or two, having a chat and then silently focusing on the TV news for a time. We are relaxed now and sleep will be long and restful, a good day and we shall head out tomorrow well restored.

After breakfast we retrace our steps from the first day by going past the Odeon and over to the left bank of the Seine and walk along the quays to the Musee D'Orsay. Whether it is by design or purely subconsciously we are definitely staying with very familiar themes on this trip.

Having said that, there really is no excuse ever needed for making a visit to this wonderful museum. The bonus today is that once again it is very quiet, in fact there is no queue but we still have to zigzag our way through the ropeway to the entrance. The lack of crowds will enable us to get unrestricted views of the most popular paintings, especially the ones by the impressionists. We will take full advantage and linger and be enthralled by these familiar but enriching works.

Your first impressions (sorry) though are dominated not by the art but by the building itself, a sympathetic and striking conversion of the old train terminal.

Unfortunately now, you are not officially allowed to take photographs of the works of art in the museum although in reality it is rarely enforced. However if you are feeling particularly law- abiding you can content yourself with

views of the architecture and today with a small number of visitors it is an ideal time to take full advantage of this very interesting structure.

The art in this museum is truly fabulous and many of the paintings are breath-taking. One such canvas, although I am sure not to everyone's taste, is a purely faithful representation of a country scene, photographic in quality. This is Rosa Bonheur's painting 'Labourage Nivernais' or 'Le Sombrage'. I have to say I always just stand in awe in front of this painting whenever I see it. It is a very large canvas, so faithfully rendered that you feel as if you are standing in the field watching the farm workers drive the massive cattle that are ploughing the land. Rosa Bonheur was one of the first female artists to break through onto the Paris art scene, exhibiting at the famous 1854 exhibition that coincided with Napoleon III upgrading himself to Emperor. She was awarded a medal at this spectacular event but this painting in the Musee D'Orsay predates this exhibition. No doubt she would have inspired an exhibition visitor, the young Berthe Morisot, the female artist so closely associated with the Impressionists and whose paintings will feature alongside the works of her male counterparts as we go around the museum.

We take our time today as it is still raining outside, enjoying a leisurely viewing of the art works. Today we are able to linger over the Impressionist paintings set in their own gallery at the top of the museum. One of the joys of this building is the way it has been stripped back to reveal the skeleton in a way. The walkways that can be used to reach the higher parts of the building give superb views of the structure. Of course a few photos of the fine station clock located above the entrance are essential and you get many photo opportunities as you negotiate your way higher and higher. Once on the top level there is one photo that always has to be taken. There is the stunning view through the large transparent clock face with the backdrop of Paris set out over the Seine leading the eye to the higher reaches of Paris on the right bank with Sacre Coeur at the summit. Even if you take this view of the clock in colour it always comes out as black and white. You just have to be patient and wait for the space to clear of people and give you the shot you require.

It is a view taken thousands of times but never fails to delight. That out of the way we carry on with the Impressionist gallery. I will not attempt to describe any individual paintings here by Monet, Renoir, Cezanne, Degas etc... but just urge you to come and I challenge you to leave uninspired as I know you will leave with your life enhanced. Please just do it.

Back outside it is a very grey and drizzly day - who says Paris is more beautiful in the rain? Well, actually perhaps it is. We wander through the Tuileries but with the rain falling steadily the ubiquitous green chairs are wet and unappealing today and we make our way to another very familiar place to us - the Musée de l'Orangerie at the far end of the gardens that overlook the Place de la Concorde. The atrocious weather conditions have just cleared slightly at this point giving an unmissable photo opportunity. The drifting cloud cover makes the Eiffel Tower appear as if it is still under construction as the top half disappears into the mist and cloud. Not a view to be missed and one of those moments when you find that you are in the right place at the right time. I have to admit that the shots I get over to the tower and around Concorde are beautiful and special; yes perhaps just that touch more beautiful in the rain.

The Orangerie we have visited many times over the years and we never tire of it. Of course it is most closely associated with Claude Monet and the massive water lily canvasses that take up the entire floor of the exhibition space. Below the Monet gallery is another fine display and again plenty of interest for those  who are in love with Impressionist art. Also today there is a more modernist exhibition of art and sculpture to view if that is more to your taste. Sadly, the painting that is my very favourite in the whole world of art is not here, having been loaned out to another exhibition – Renoir's 'Jeunes filles au piano' (Girls at the piano). For me this is just the most exquisite representation of everything the painters of the period were trying to achieve – a true masterpiece and my 'desert island' work of art.

Our art fix over it is still raining outside but we gain a little shelter as we walk down the tree lined space along the right bank of the river and cross over the Seine to the left bank and make our way back to our hotel. We are so wet by now that we decide to see if the Jardins du Luxembourg are also more beautiful in the rain. Sadly, they are not, and what is definitely more appealing is a long hot shower and that we decide to head quickly to the hotel to arrange.

Refreshed, we tonight head out into the Paris evening in search of a restaurant. Unusually for me I have no pre-set plans and not even had a peruse of TripAdvisor to check out the area. We do not want to walk far tonight so we will have to use all our instincts to choose a suitable venue.

As we walk to the end of the gardens on the Boulevard Saint Michel I passed a man sitting on the pavement begging. I carry on by. I have to say that I rarely give money to people on the streets; I suppose in my mind I am a little cynical as to what they will use the money for. It is a fine line between helping someone and feeding a destructive habit. As I move along by him just out of the corner of my eye I see that he has a young girl with him aged no more than 5 or 6 years of age. This is the same age as my beautiful granddaughter and I cannot help noticing that this poor young girl is no less beautiful. I turn around unable to continue on my way and in the best French I can muster I explain to him that on this occasion I am compelled to leave something but only if he will promise to spend it on the child. He says that he will and I have to trust him to do so but the whole scene is heartbreaking.

Sadly this is not unusual now on the streets of Paris.

Just around the corner across the street we spy a bistro, very traditional looking and we are drawn over to take a look. We have only walked about five hundred yards from the hotel and for tonight it feels quite far enough. The bistro is the Brasserie Royal Luxembourg at 5 Rue Gay-Lussac. It is a welcoming restaurant that serves traditional bistro fare with a nod to the Basque area of south west France. We are the only diners and this is not usually a good sign.

Generally I would avoid entering an empty restaurant but the owners give us a pleasant smiling welcome and I am always encouraged by any restaurant that chalks up a plat du jour. We settle at a table and drinks are readily forthcoming and I try one from the selection of Basque beers from the old bar. The beer is cold and refreshing. The food is fine, nothing fancy, the portions are perhaps over generous but the dishes have plenty of flavour. We are happy to sit quietly and enjoy the peace and solitude broken only by one more customer that evening who goes to sit near the bar and passes the odd word with the chef when he comes out front of house.

We have covered a lot of ground today and re-acquainted ourselves with familiar parts of Paris and in particular its art and culture. We are tired and satisfied and wave a goodbye and head in the direction of our hotel. My mind is still full of the encounter with the father and child and for some reason I hope they are still there at the corner of the street. Why, I do not know, because I can do nothing more, she cannot come home with us but nonetheless I hope they are there. They are not and I do hope that at least this evening her father has treated her. I of course can carry on my comfortable life but tonight sleep will be elusive as her lovely face is fixed in my mind. I can't help but feel as I write this that it sounds somewhat patronising and I don't wish it to do so and hope it comes across in the way that it genuinely affected me that evening. It moved me, but it also made me feel guilty but thankful about my lot in life but frustratingly helpless as a tourist. I still think of her and I hope they have made progress from the street and on to a meaningful life. It also raises the appalling paradox of on the one hand I am in a city where so many need help and comfort but all the while there are others that are set on a course of hate to kill and destroy.

Love never fails.

The next day we are meeting John and Elizabeth, our friends from California and I will recount that encounter separately in the next chapter.

After that day with our friends we headed home. It has been a trip that has been quite different to any other. Paris has undeniably changed and I defy anyone to contradict that. It has not got quite the same light-hearted joy and ambiance as before but as time passes that will surely return. It is very quiet compared to previous visits and the people are genuinely glad to see you, pleased that the dreadful events of recent times have not deterred us. They are unaware of how close we came to cancelling our visit and I feel a bit of a fraud in accepting their thanks.

One thing that has surprised us is the apparent lack of any extra security, it must surely be there but on the streets it feels just as it always did. There is the odd policeman passing by and high level buildings still have the usual visible gun security but nothing more seems to have been added. Only on the very final walk before getting the bus to the Gare du Nord do we see anything more intense. In front of Notre Dame a group of heavily armed soldiers come by and their gaze sweeps the scene, looking intently around them.

One of the soldiers is a young girl, surely

barely twenty years old but armed to the teeth – that is a striking and shocking image. Have they been dispatched to the square because of some possible threat? It is probable but life goes on, and we enjoy a last look around. After these days back in Paris I no longer have any fear, quite the reverse now. Paris is slowly recovering and I have enjoyed it and we have made some more memories to add to the past ones in the finest city in the world.

There is a postscript to my new found confidence. We left the Gare du Nord on the Eurostar for London at around 2.30 that afternoon and about thirty minutes later the train station was closed for a security alert and trains were cancelled until late that night. We had just avoided it and completed our trip without incident – just.

LONG DISTANCE
FRIENDS

We love spending time together in Paris as a couple as I am sure do most people. Paris is a romantic destination for many as witnessed by the padlocks entangled on the Pont des Arts. You will probably have gathered by now that one of the great pleasures for me is that of going with or meeting friends in Paris and sharing the experience. I will return to that theme as the book draws to a close. When we look back over the many times we have spent in this wonderful city it is the visits with friends that have provided the most enduring and precious memories. One such occasion was a little more unusual and unexpected than any of the others.

A few years into our travels around France and Paris I found myself drawn to replying to some enquiries on Trip Advisor regarding places and things to see and do in France and in particular Provence, Burgundy, Paris and anything wine themed. It was very satisfying to be helpful. When you got a reply that said how much they had appreciated the information and used it on a trip I was pleased to have shared what we had discovered. One of those replies started a friendship that has endured to today. The Trip Advisor travel friendship agency worked its magic.

Initially I provided some information about Burgundy and Paris to a fellow traveller from California. He used that on a visit to France and then asked more questions about the areas that had been raised due to experiencing them in person. This email conversation soon expanded outside of the general sphere of travels to France and we found we had a good deal in common.

We started to share our thoughts on family and other interests although I found his appreciation of the English game of cricket frustratingly non-existent, but I cured that defect. We were certainly from different backgrounds and you could say that although we both spoke English there were obvious cultural differences, cricket being the major one for me. The contact developed into a genuine friendship and soon we were sharing thoughts generally reserved to people knowing each other face to face over many years. A long distance trusting friendship had developed. This continued back and forth by e-mail for about eight years before we finally had the opportunity to meet up.

Niamh would not fly that long distance to California but John and Elizabeth have no qualms about racking up frequent flyer miles and were coming over on a short tour of England. We decided to travel from Lancashire and meet up at Hidcote Manor Gardens in the Cotswolds, a very beautiful garden that we had wanted to visit for some time.

The day arrived and for us the journey was a bit traumatic. Our car was broken into – at a National Trust property of all places. We finally arrived on the Hidcote car park with one side of our car taped up with yellow and black tape – what an entrance. We had a great day together and it was such a pleasure to meet up and continue as if we had been friends for life. After visiting the gardens which were a great delight to them we enjoyed lunch in Chipping Campden before ending our day and first meeting, a day that had been all too short. Our friendship however was sealed.

A couple of years later they visited Paris for a few days and I have told the torturous story of how we eventually arrived in Paris at the same time in the previous 'Bataclan' chapter. We arranged to meet at the Panthéon but as we walked up towards the building I heard a voice call out from the opposite side of the road and we all risked the traffic to meet up again in a joyous reunion.

We decided on a plan of action for our day together and the first port of call for a photo was on the steps of the church of St Etienne du Mont, Place Sainte-Geneviève, the 'Midnight in Paris' steps. From there we headed to Rue Descartes where we stopped at the restaurant La Maison de Verlaine. Here there is the plaque on the entrance wall referring to Hemingway having used a room there to write in peace back in his Paris days of the 1920's. Hemingway always appeals to Americans. John had a real desire to experience Rue Mouffetard, the vibrant market street in this part of the Latin Quarter. It was an inspired choice and we were like two kids in a sweet shop as we took in the delights of this amazing street.

John would have his favourite shops and call me over, I would inevitably take him to the incredible fishmongers and purr with delight at all the fresh fruits of the sea on offer; a display unlike anything I could possibly find back home. The girls obviously were drawn to quite  different shops and we left them to discover the street at their own pace.

The delight in sharing an experience like this in Paris is difficult to convey but if you have someone with you to excitedly bounce the discoveries off each other then it is one of life's great joys. We finally dragged ourselves away from the bustling market street and headed into Jardin des Plantes, a very fine and important garden in the city. The day sadly was dull with a fine drizzle but it did not stop our enjoyment of the plants and buildings in this large well tendered space but a visit to the zoo was not on the agenda. When we emerged onto the riverside we were blessed with a fabulous view back towards Notre Dame and the islands, an area that John and Elizabeth are very fond of. We walked slowly, savouring our time together and finding out that we could all talk so very easily and freely. Lunch inevitably was on Rue Saint-Louis en l'Île and it was a long and convivial one.

Our friendship was facing our first test but John was understanding and patient. You may be aware of the English obsession with soccer and although I no longer live in the North of England my loyalty is to the team I have supported since childhood and that is the town where I was born - Blackburn. During our lunch they were playing the final game of a dreadfully poor season and the outcome would determine if they were to be relegated to a lower division. I was surreptitiously following events on my iPhone I am ashamed to admit and the outcome of the game was in the balance. At one point it seemed they would survive the relegation but defeat was snatched from the jaws of victory and all that faint hope disappeared. My sad face had to be painted with a fixed smile. I recovered and concentrated on my friends. Our soccer obsession has a lot to answer for but after all the conversations I had had over the years with John he understood completely.

We took Elizabeth along the street to Berthillon Ice cream parlour and treated her to an ice cream. I feel that she would have made the trip from California just for that such was her joy at this treat. This was such a simple shared experience but one that means so much in its own way.

It was getting close  to the time when we would have to part and we sat and talked for a while in the park behind Notre Dame, one of John and Elizabeth's favourite spots. The weather had improved and a gentle sun streamed through the trees. An acoustic guitar was played softly in the corner of the park and three small children were playing happily in front of us. It was a perfect end to a memorable day. We agreed to meet again somewhere down the line and since then we have made the future arrangements.

The point of my story is really to emphasise that if you make the effort and immerse yourself in the people and places of your travels then you can reap many benefits and some from the most unexpected sources. We can travel throughout France where now there are people we can call on in so many parts of the country and spend time with them as friends; you cannot put a price on that. Yes, I know there are times when we all need a quiet, relaxing break with no distractions and not too much social interaction but please get out there in France and meet the people, you will not regret it.

THE LAST TIME
WE SAW PARIS

T his is an account of a very personal journey that we made to Paris a few years ago. It is not strictly speaking our last time in Paris by any means but it was a special visit with dear friends. Very sadly this cannot ever be repeated and so for us in an all too real and meaningful sense it is the last time we saw Paris in such a way. I have written this in quite a loose personal style and I hope that the affection I have for my friends and for Paris shines through. It was a very special time - the best of times. Names have been changed to protect the guilty.

The long and wonderful evening we spent at

Le Hide Restaurant on Rue du General Lanrezac just around the corner from the Arc de Triomphe was sadly drawing to a close. The time spent at the table had stretched to around four hours and this had been a joyous and unforgettable occasion for the eight subscribers of our member's only village wine club – actually just our cottage dining room. Roman, our generous and delightful waiter who kept us entertained all evening with his patient, limitless good humour moved across the floor to present us with our extensive bill.

"Roman, mais non, nous avons l'Armagnac pour tout" said James or words to that effect.

Roman, heavy eyes already wanting to drift off to sleep, simply hooked his collar onto the coat rack and feigned a deep restful sleep. Somewhere, anywhere but still serving les Anglais in the cosy restaurant.

His final act was a perfect reply to our determination to squeeze every last moment from this unforgettable night.

This gathering was one of many occasions on

this short trip that reminded you of the unique joy of being in Paris with lifelong friends.

The journey had all started at the train station in the North of England two days earlier. Our merry band gathered to wait for the Virgin train to London and then on to St Pancras for the Eurostar to Paris.

There was Richard and Kirsten, Richard as always was annoyingly wide awake so early in the morning and making us all laugh as we arrived onto the station platform. Kirsten of course disowned his every utterance and gesture.

Myself and Niamh complete with our very small suitcase that was crammed with the essentials for a Paris weekend. James and Joan and Nick of course, tour organisers. Desmond was there just emerging from WH Smiths with his newspaper, a necessary companion to give him just a little more to worry about. Pickford's removals had just dropped off Natasha's luggage for the weekend and had just gone back to their house for the rest.

She looked and pointed in total astonishment at Niamh's suitcase, Niamh's one small suitcase.

How could we both possibly travel with so little? Well we could and we did and poor Des had to attend to the extensive heavy supplies on the journey to Paris.

Poor Des. Anyway, once he has packed the luggage onto the train we can set off and within about three hours we are checked in at St Pancras and ready for Paris. All of us are as excited as a bunch of schoolchildren as usual and our anticipation level is very high. Time for a coffee, no one has gone to the Champagne Bar on the Eurostar platform this time, maybe it is just that little too early even for us.

The part of the station dedicated to the Eurostar is a fine example of how to sympathetically restore an old building and it is worth taking a stroll around the concourse before boarding the Eurostar. The two statues of 'The Lovers' and of John Betjamin are fine pieces of art. Overlooking the scene there is the large 'Dent' clock and of course the superb arched glass roof. It is very much ancient meets modern but architecturally it is extremely well accomplished.

On this trip Nick has done us proud by obtaining Premium tickets at very little extra cost in relation to the standard train fare. This ensures a meal with wine and a touch more space enabling us to be able to sit as a party at table seats.

Richard is in his element here and his repartee with the stewardesses begins to pay off almost immediately. His fawning excess of compliments is proving irresistible and by the time we reach Paris he has gathered enough of one glass size bottles of wine to ensure he will never need to use the mini bar at the hotel other than to keep his wine chilled. The stewardesses somehow never seemed to realise just how much extra wine they had brought to the table and this was something only Richard could have got away with. Flatter a different one every time seemed to be his strategy and it worked a treat. It has to be said that the food was pretty grim but we hoped for better in Paris of course.

After arriving at the Gare du Nord station in Paris we took the Metro to reach the Hotel Balmoral located close to the Arc de Triomphe. The Metro was packed and we all stayed close to our luggage, wallets and purses. It was relatively cool down below ground and as we started to emerge onto the Champs-Élysées the intense heat felt as if you were entering a large oven. We paused at the top of the steps to take in the surroundings and look at the Arc de Triomphe so that we could be certain that we were actually in Paris and the fun could begin.

There was a certain degree of consultation and Google searching before we could make our way with any certainty to the hotel but we did eventually arrive without losing anyone along the way. The hotel was beautiful and it was difficult to believe that we had obtained this quality at the price. The welcome at the reception desk was kind and efficient and then Niamh had to face her ultimate French crisis – the lift.

This fine example was I think from the Belle Époque and incredibly small, a tiny broom cupboard set in a lift shaft. I reassured Niamh about the odds of this contraption plummeting to earth and she closed her eyes as the five second journey passed off without incident. Our small but perfectly formed room had the classic Parisian view from a Juliet balcony allowing you to look both ways along the lively street. Perfect. All the white faced buildings reflected the gorgeous light of this hot day and the old wrought iron balconies down both sides of the street took you back to another era but most certainly in Paris.

Showered and refreshed we all gathered for our first foray out into the warm Parisian evening for our first meal. We were all tired so we were not looking for a restaurant that was too fancy or expensive. We walked away from the Arc de Triomphe and reached the junction of the Avenue des Ternes where we quickly agreed on an attractive classic brasserie and were warmly welcomed and seated at a large table looking over the boulevard.

The meal was very enjoyable, nothing too elaborate, just good honest bistro food and we all relaxed into our Parisian tourist mode. Des unfortunately did have a certain amount of stress as he was determined to have a bottle of Badoit with his meal. Niamh and I have previous on this issue having gone through an international incident on the subject of Badoit in Auxerre. I said to Des he would be lucky to get Badoit and indeed it seemed as if it would never arrive at the table. Finally, after an interminable delay Des's precious Badoit finally arrived at the table and his little face lit up. Its only water surely – isn't it?

When the desserts arrived I glanced down the table just in time to snap a photograph of James with a smile that reminded you of a little child receiving a tube of Smarties or M & M's – his Îles flottantes had arrived.

It was a beautiful balmy night and even though we were all pretty tired we strolled up to the Arc de Triomphe which was bathed in light with the twinkling Eiffel Tower lighting up the night sky beyond. We took in the Paris night time ambiance for a while before it was clear that we all needed some sleep.

We all slept well.

Gathering in the morning down in reception we were surprised to find Desmond and Natasha emerging from a secret door set into the wooden panelled wall. What was behind this Platinum level door? We needed to find out – did  they have some master suite in there and we poor peasants a mere standard room? We were allowed a tour and no it was not the honeymoon suite but it was certainly finer and larger than everybody else's. Nick, why this favouritism?

Today I was in tour guide mode and planned a history trip for our party to the Marais, one of my most favourite parts of Paris. We emerged from the Metro station at Pont Marie, the bridge that joins the Right Bank to the Ile Saint-Louis. Our merry band of history lovers (well they soon will be) started our tour at the Hotel de Sens. This historic monument is now an art library but originally the Paris residence of the Archbishop of Sens. It has a cannonball lodged in its walls that resulted from one of the many usual protests by the populace in Paris.

Going through Le village Saint-Paul and in front of the large and stark Paroisse Saint Paul church we crossed Rue de Rivoli and found the lovely square of Place Sainte Catherine. This peaceful tree lined square houses many restaurants and cafes including Au Bistrot de la Place whose image adorns many a table mat.

A place to linger but tour guides do not linger so off we all go following my lead back onto the Rue Rivoli. It is a short walk down Rue Rivoli until you find the Hotel de Sully which now in fact is used as government offices but you are allowed to walk through the doorway corridor that connects to the garden beyond. This pretty space is a lovely precursor to the main event that is reached by a small entrance gap on the far corner – Place de Vosges.

This is perhaps the high point that sets the standard for public spaces in Paris. An incredibly symmetrical place formed by the grand houses set along all four sides that were built in the 17th Century for Henry IV. Until the Revolution it was THE meeting place for the French aristocracy and the interconnecting rooms of what was in effect a grand square palace led to much secret intrigue. I finally allow the tourists a break and is there any better place to sit than in the centre of this amazing square. I don't think that deep thought crossed anyone's mind – they just wanted a rest.

I encourage a stroll around the perimeter and all have to agree this is well worthwhile with many fashionable shops, cafes and restaurants on the walk around the sheltered courtyard.

The very high end L'Ambroisie restaurant has its entrance on the perimeter walkway. We pass on lunch here despite Richard's protest that nothing is too good for Kirsten and head back into the Marais. Outside there is the most beautiful former Patisserie decorated in Art Nouveau style that sadly is now used as a fashion shop.

This business played a part in helping many of the oppressed residents of the Marias to survive during the occupation of Paris during the war when this area was more than any other targeted for harassment and deportation. The baker here secretly made more bread than he was permitted to do and distributed it to ones in dire need in the Marais. A brave man, but part of a group of many that tried to alleviate the suffering. This gorgeous frontage is still used in many films that are set in Paris and is probably one of the last with such an original feature.

We walked down Rue des Francs Bourgeois, a fashionable street allowing many more opportunities for shopping in the tempting variety of independent shops. Clothes, shoes, handbags, perfume and so on were here to the ladies delight – Richard ran off into the far distance, hand securing his wallet in his back pocket.

We eventually found him in the grounds of the Musee Carnavalet halfway down the street, sitting alone in the garden, head in hands.

The Carnavalet would be a good museum for another cultural experience but I think most have had sufficient culture for one day. It would be cheaper for Richard though but even he accepted that the fate of his wallet was sealed.

The Marais, due to its eclectic mix of people,

is a very interesting and stimulating place to explore. Its relatively recent history is primarily as a location where the Jews settled and lived and traded. It is also the scene of their deportations during the Second World War, a despicable event that almost completely emptied the area of Jews and other 'undesirables'.

There are poignant reminders of that tragic time that you will find as you start working your way down the side streets. One of the most heart-breaking is on the wall of  the Lycee Victor Hugo on Rue De Sevigne and commemorates the loss of 500 pupils from that school – yes, I had to look more than twice, 500 - at the hands of the Gestapo. The sign also acknowledges the willing collaboration of the French Authorities. There are other plaques on the schools in this area of the Marais, none escaped the evil attentions of the occupiers.

The area still gives the visitor a sense of the Jewishness of this part of Paris with the Kosher food on offer and some dedicated shops. It is more mixed in culture in these times and especially with the western end of the Marais now being very much a gay quarter.

We do the full circle of the Marais and head back towards the Place de Vosges and settle down for lunch at the restaurant Royal Turenne close to the square. This turns out to be

an ideal choice – a proper French brasserie with the waiters all correctly attired – aprons around the waist. The food is good and all of us are served except Niamh who is left as the only one still staring at a place mat much to Richard's amusement. Her meal did eventually come but it was a close run thing.

It was a lovely location and we were sat in front of the old bar, fully stocked in the usual Parisian manner – very atmospheric.

It was decided that we all wanted to go over to the Islands and specifically the Ile Saint-Louis and the stroll is not too far, taking you across one of the many bridges straddling the Seine at this point. The views both ways down the Seine are memorable and we stand on the bridge for a while to soak in this extensive view of the Paris skyline bathed in warm bright sunlight.

The Ile Saint-Louis is a wonderful mix of designer shops, food shops and a great variety of restaurants. One of these of course is the Café Med which holds special memories as we ate here as a group on a previous visit – a very memorable lunch that ended with Kirsten lining up all our wine glasses for a photo – and there were so many that it needed a panoramic setting on the camera.

As you move towards the bridge that links the island with the larger one - Ile de la Cite - we get fabulous views of the quaysides and the people strolling as couples or walking their dogs. All Parisians have a dog - usually one to carry around in their handbag. Word of advice – don't buy second hand handbags in the Paris flea markets.

Today there are many people sun-bathing on the quays and we watch the crowded river boats passing the islands and we are unable to resist returning a wave to the passengers.

We head back by Metro to the hotel to prepare for the evening and a return to the Ile Saint Louis for what will certainly be, food wise, exceptional, maybe arguably the finest and most enjoyable evening we ever had on our travels as a group. I exclude the evening on the Seine to celebrate James and Joan's 40th anniversary – we must keep the comparison fair.

Tonight we dine at Le Relais de L'Isle restaurant,

one that is run apparently by just two people, a man and wife team. It is sadly no longer there after they retired although Niamh and I did have the opportunity to revisit the following year. It was at the time of our visit the number one restaurant in Paris on Trip Advisor, comfortably beating all the fancy restaurants that Paris could muster. This was a small place with just a few downstairs tables and a small mezzanine. At the far end and sharing the bar space was a piano.

The meal was astonishingly good and all served by this one woman who kept up a blistering pace between the tables and kitchen and still having time to have a pleasant word with the diners. As the meal got underway the piano was occupied by an accomplished but quite stout pianist, just able to squeeze into the tiny space. He launched into a Beatles repertoire. Could James have asked for anything more? As the meal drew to a close he and a couple of others joined in on an impromptu karaoke.

The atmosphere and the whole experience of the evening could not really have been surpassed – but we would have another meal at Le Hide as previously mentioned at the end of the stay that would run it close.

My experience of this wonderful night was

slightly different to the others in the party. I was seated close to the last table by the door. This was occupied by a lone diner who was in a state of some emotional turmoil. He also wanted to unload this turmoil on me and did so for most of the evening. He told the story that he had been away from the States on a secondment to a country in Africa on behalf of the US Government and had been treated very badly. He said he had paid his own way to get out of Africa and was missing home and his family. I was a captive hearing ear but it was not pleasant to sit next to someone unloading like that and breaking into tears at certain points. He gave the impression that he would have questions to answer on his return. Whether his story was true, who knows? It was a bit of a surreal experience – joy on one side and tears when I turned back.

Ours was a very happy party and we bid our farewells to Madam and there were joyful hugs all round as we spilled out into the street and the Paris night.

It had been an experience that would be unforgettable and we still had late night Paris to enjoy as we strolled across the bridge to the Île de la Cité and into the square in front of Notre Dame Cathedral. In the square there was a man entertaining the crowd by performing some pyrotechnics that turned him into a human firework display.

This lit up the area in front of the Cathedral and was quite a spectacular sight that we enjoyed before heading to the Metro station and a deep sleep back at the hotel to be ready for another day.

This morning Joan had wanted to head to Montmartre and follow in the footsteps of the artists and performers of that village and take in the sights and spectacular views from the Sacre Coeur. I have to be honest that having visited Montmartre before it is not really my most favourite part of Paris. It can be a bit touristy to say the least and parts of it are a little uninviting and as you know it is the only place in Paris where someone tried to mug me.

We took the Funicular railway to the top near to the Basilica (one of Niamh's very favourite modes of transport - NOT).

At the top the views over Paris are stunning and evocative. The foreground seems little changed from old photographs but in the far distance you can see how modern Paris has evolved. Sadly, the skies are grey and threatening as we move on into Place Tertre, away from the poor aroma around this dazzling white monstrosity. In this square there are many of the sights you associate with Montmartre, the artist vying for your business and especially drawing the ubiquitous caricature. Also you recognize a restaurant or two that have adorned many a photograph and table mat, particularly La Mere Catherine. This area although touristy is a part of Montmartre I enjoy, for if you look up you can see that the signage and architecture has retained its character. This is true as you head out of the square and start to wind your way down the Butte.

We reach the Moulin Rouge and easily resist buying tickets for tonight's performance – I am in any case nearly run over by an angry Parisian cyclist who feels I am occupying his space on the pavement. Whatever! In any case it is starting to feel a bit seedy and unfriendly in this area and so we all decide to head for the Metro and go over to the Eiffel Tower quarter and partake of lunch.

Unknown to us the heavens have opened whilst we are underground and we (well me) make the fatal mistake of making everyone emerge from the station at the Pont Alexandre, a place that is totally exposed to the elements and has the wide open space of the Esplanade des Invalides in front of you. The only thing we can do is as quickly as possible get across the park and into the side streets leading around to the tower and gain a modicum of shelter in the doorways. I hear the words 'Paris is more beautiful in the rain' coming out of my mouth but quickly slam it shut. Sadly, finding a suitable restaurant is not proving that easy and we all get wet, very wet. Eventually we run into a bistro - Le Recrutement Café, 36, Boulevard La Tour Maubourg - leaving a trail of water behind in the reception and puddles form beneath our table. We were as Blackadder would have said 'wetter than a fully clothed wet thing that had sat longingly in a deep wet place.'

It was somewhat bizarre to be sat in the restaurant with the rain pouring down and yet all the full length windows pulled back fully open – it was wet but yet extremely warm. We were steaming in a literal sense, rain clouds forming above our heads in the damp warm atmosphere of the restaurant.

It was a very good lunch, basic hearty bistro fare that was just what was needed when you are soaked to the skin and hungry.

The clouds parted, the weather cleared and the

sun shone as we left the restaurant but we looked bedraggled, our clothes now shapeless and hanging damp and limp but drying now a little more quickly in the hot sun.

The sky was bright enough now to encourage us to head to the Eiffel Tower and we made our way along the street towards the Champs des Mars. The tower has lost none of its magic for any of us although most of us are very familiar now with this majestic sight.

You cannot help but be impressed every time you come here and we head through its pillars and walk over to the Trocadero where you gain arguably the finest view of this monu-ment looking through it to the area around Les Invalides.

On the Trocadero there are many African traders trying to tempt you to buy one of their tax free goodies but we resist. I am still damp and feel very scruffy and unwashed and I think that is probably how most of us feel so the fairly short walk back to the hotel to freshen up is the best option.

Niamh and I are made of sterner stuff (or just crazy) and after a very quick shower we take the Metro to our favourite housewares shop – E Dehillerin – a famous Parisian institution. This is the store we visited on a previous trip and bought a steel frying pan and I now wanted another to go with it. On that last occasion our friend Ian said 'I was hyperactive.' I was quite proud of that assessment and still am.

Dehillerin store is for me 'kid in a sweet shop' stuff.

A very old fashioned place that has everything and I do mean everything for the French kitchen. I particularly love going down the winding steps to the basement where you feel as if you are rummaging in their stock room. Your purchases are written on a chitty and you take that to a till at an old wooden desk and there you pay and take away your hand written receipt. A very atmospheric place and a store that takes you back in time as regards service and display.

Back at the hotel everybody was gathered in the reception area for our final night out, one last superb meal before we head home tomorrow.

Before the meal we sit for a while on the terrace

of a bar just around the corner from our hotel. Richard orders a quite unusual Belgian beer that I have my doubts about. As I suspected he hates it and continues to moan long enough for Kirsten to decide it is preferable to swap her glass of wine with him and stop the droning sound. She knows how to make Richard happy.

Tonight's meal has been booked just down the street from the hotel at a restaurant that comes highly recommended – Le Hide. This is the restaurant that I described at the outset and the evening was long and did not disappoint – a truly memorable evening.

We arrived and bundled our way into the restaurant, Richard as usual needing to make a good first impression. Almost immediately he had swapped coats with Roman, a man he had only just met, as he felt he was actually the one dressed appropriately as a waiter and encouraged Roman to take a seat at the table and Richard would wait on the tables. We all just said good evening as you do and pretended he was dining alone.

The menu was short but full of good things – just how we like a menu to be presented. I was sitting next to Des and he had some very garlicky snails, they smelt delicious but snails are still something I have avoided eating in France so far. I had salt marsh lamb and so did some of the others but everyone was very impressed with the quality of the food. Wine continued to flow and we enjoyed some wonderful selections of French wines that were very nearly in Richard's price range.

The conversation did not slow down for a moment, even when eating and Roman sensed our mood and played up to it throughout the evening and added so much to the general banter around the table. The other diners must surely have thought that we were just crazy English. I have the feeling this is a quiet romantic restaurant as a rule – not tonight it isn't.

The chef curiously enough is Japanese but he cooks with a total regard for classic French cookery and his food was sublime. To end the meal he had one dish on the menu that was completely irresistible – an assiette of small desserts with coffee that was so tempting that we all ordered it. A sight to see to have the entire table eating the same plate – it was delicious.

The dessert rounded off the most amazing meal and an evening of bonhomie that will never be forgotten.

Roman then performed his party piece with the coat rack and that could not have summed up the mood of that evening any better.

Was it to be rated finer than the meal on the Island – who cares – both were just incredible nights and neither restaurant we felt could have improved on the experience they gave us – perfect.

We said our goodbyes to Roman and made our way on to the Champs-Élysées, chiefly to use the loos at McDonalds. Everyone stumbled back out without purchasing a happy meal and it was the most pleasant of strolls back to the hotel on a beautiful balmy night after the best of times together.

Next morning we started off down the Champs-Élysées – this time for Richard and his wallet there was to be no escape – we had to pass the perfume store Sephora and Richard and I had to go inside by Kirsten and Niamh's command.

Richard was totally unprepared for this despite having known about his wedding anniversary for 25 years. At the Sephora store leading from the entrance you are confronted with a long and gently sloping ramp giving the sensation that you may be going into a stadium which I suppose to a certain degree you are. Along both sides of this ramp there are a multitude of glamourous store assistants poised and ready to squirt you with any number of fragrances. After negotiating that you then emerge into this cavernous and apparently underground space where you will soon be aware that if they have not got Kirsten's favourite perfume, lotion, eau de cologne etc... then it doesn't exist. It is a store that will test the limit on Richard's credit cards.

I am not sure how many times Richard was 'squirted' as he ran the gauntlet but he is eventually in the inner sanctum. It is for Kirsten an enjoyable moment – to be treated in such a way - and Richard apparently goes along with this with fairly good grace. He is delighted to have made such a contribution to Kirsten's happiness on her special day. It is only when he gets outside that he realised just how expensively he had been mugged.

We strolled on toward the Place de la Concorde, going across and into the Tuileries Garden on what was a beautiful sunny Paris morning. The gardens were fairly quiet and a joy to be there, meandering around the fountain and pond and to take in the atmosphere of this finest of gardens – a favourite place.

We all feel that it is time for a coffee and we make the mistake of sitting at a café in the Tuileries forgetting that there is a 200% premium on the price for the privilege of sitting and enjoying the view. The most expensive coffee I have ever had but never mind it was a lovely moment and we savoured it as long as we could.

The Louvre looks stunningly impressive on such a morning and the scene as you look around the vast square with the glass pyramid at its centre is quite breath-taking.

It is a fitting end to the sightseeing part of the trip and the Louvre is always an unforgettable part of this wonderful City.

With food as always constantly on our minds we go over onto the right bank and stroll around the streets close to the Louvre and Rue Rivoli and settle on one that although on a fairly busy street does look to be an inviting bistro. So it proves.

The superb juicy and perfectly cooked steaks are so good that Des cannot bring himself to stop eating for a final photo call and his eating process is captured for all time.

And so the most wonderful of trips draws to a close and we reluctantly make our way back to the hotel, collect our cases and head to the Gare du Nord.

There are thanks all round to Joan and Nick for the work that has gone into organizing these fabulous few days and we are a happy weary band of friends that leave Paris well satisfied.

Why was it so wonderful – why did the trip work so well as a group?

I can do no better than quote a passage from Pride & Prejudice and let Jane Austen have the final say:

'Enjoyment was certain – that of suitableness as companions: a suitableness which comprehended health and temper to bear inconveniences – a cheerfulness to enhance every pleasure – and affection and intelligence, which might supply it among themselves if there were disappointments abroad.'

JOURNEY'S END
IN PARIS –

a long Weekend heading Home

This chapter is a fairly complete account of one particular trip and with that in mind I have tried to tell the story in the form of a blog or diary style and I hope you enjoy this style of writing. It is a trip that we made at the end of a stay in Perpignan in South West France and it was a delightful end to a very special journey to two places that mean a lot to us. Here we are at the Gare de Lyon on:

Friday 23rd September

Paris, Île-de-France, France

We arrived in Paris right on time having made up a 15mins delay on the TGV from Perpignan. The large station concourse at Gare de Lyon was absolutely packed with people leaving the capital for the weekend. Almost finding ourselves stepping over them and trying to avoid running over hurrying feet with our heavy suitcase we eventually made it out of the station into the bright late summer sun. It looked like everyone in Paris was in a hurry to get home after work or head to the coast for the weekend to take full advantage of the wonderful weather. We made the sensible decision to walk to our hotel that is located at the start of the long Rue Rivoli – Paris Rivoli Hotel – not even wanting to try to fight our way down the crowded escalators to the Metro lines.

We arrived at the hotel looking rather the worse for wear and the hotel looks fine. It is in a terrific location just about 5mins walking distance from the L'Isle St Louis and on the fringe of the heart of the Marais, a part of Paris we always enjoy and one that is full of interest both historically and culturally.

Our Thierry Henry look-alike receptionist is nattily dressed and super-efficient and gives us a warm but slightly supercilious welcome. For some strange reason he seems to find us a quite amusing couple of Les Anglais and a great foil for his humorous expressions and especially his obsession with trying to catch us out in our use of the French language. Is it us or just the English in general? From this first moment of meeting our friend we cannot pass him by (he is always there) without being the object of his amusement. We feel as if we are bit players in a film or French farce and we are part of the comedic script but we take it in good part but always with the hope that someone else is to be found on duty or we just try to run past the desk as quickly as possible.

The hotel room is very comfortable and quiet, overlooking an old courtyard backing onto a restaurant terrace. Another tall hotel has its entrance on the rue behind. A quick shower is essential and we then head for the Islands, tentatively edging past our friend who no doubt thinks we are going to get lost out there and will have to ring him for a rescue plan.

It is so good to be here and the city of Paris looks superb in the subdued early evening light. We stop on the Pont Louis-Phillippe leading over to the Island to take some photos of the riverscape.

Is there a more beautiful city than this with the river Seine meandering calmly, gently lit boats coming under the bridge in both directions, alive with the contented murmur of passengers and the sun setting over the magnificent skyline of the architecture of the Islands? I conclude with some certainty that there is not and we have struck it rich to be here in Paris with

such fabulous late summer weather.

Firstly tonight our plan is to take a stroll on the Pont Saint Louis and absorb the view across to Notre Dame and then move back over to the L'Isle St Louis beyond the ancient

cathedral. Some tuneful buskers are performing in the balmy early evening and very pleasant it is to stand there on the bridge for a few minutes and absorb the calming ambiance of the scene. Our favourite street on the islands is Rue St Louis en L'Isle and we meander slowly down it specifically taking in the restaurants so as to make a choice for our dining tonight. We are not desiring anything too fancy as it has been a long travelling day and we are tired but we decide that we are sensible to at least reserve one, Le Relais en L'Isle for the coming weekend in case they get fully booked. We had dined here the previous year and had a truly fabulous evening, so we really wanted to go back again.

The lady who runs the front of house, incredibly on her own, was just inside the entrance and busy as usual but I got her attention. I asked for a table for Saturday night but no, she was 'complet'.

Sad face!

I asked for Sunday but again it was a no, totally booked again.

Even sadder faces!

In fact she said she was booked up until 8th October over two weeks away. The power of TripAdvisor and being No1.

Thinking on my feet I said - 'what about tonight'?

She went back to her large black book and flicked quickly through and soon came back to say a couple who had reserved a table were late in arriving so there was a chance of a cancellation.

'Come back in 10 mins' - and she firmly took my

arm and showed me the appointed time on my watch to make sure I knew when we had to return.

'You will come back won't you'? she said.

We assured her that we would most definitely return and in fact we didn't go far from the restaurant, just out of her eye line. As soon as the 10mins were up we went back inside and were so happy when she sat us at the still empty table.

This establishment is not No:1 on T/A for nothing. There are very good reasons why it beats all the Michelin starred restaurants even though it only has one person looking after the ten or so tables. I suspect there is but a solitary chef as well, most probably her husband. Why is it so highly rated – it is the location for one, the ambiance with the pianist playing soft jazz in the cramped recess under the small mezzanine, the incredible level of service that I still cannot fathom how she manages to achieve but most of all of course the quality of the food. We are in for another memorable treat tonight without a doubt.

Madam had in fact remembered the two of us from our visit last year when we were part of what I am afraid to say was quite a loud party of eight and she was clearly delighted that she had been able to offer us a table. The feeling was entirely mutual. So to the menu for the evening - we chose smoked salmon with apple, avocado and tomato for starter and that was zinging with freshness – gorgeous. After that I was served a juicy, quite rare pave of steak with Roquefort sauce and pomme dauphinoise. Niamh chose the fresh sea bream and she loved that. As a measure of the skill of the talented chef my steak was rested to perfection and was served precisely rare as I had asked. Niamh could not stretch her appetite to a dessert but I had a 'flaming' crème caramel that took a long time before the flames died down after madam had ignited the Armagnac soaked bowl at the table. Madam whispered to Niamh that she would bring her an extra spoon and I reluctantly allowed a couple of mouthfuls to be taken from my prized dessert.

To accompany the meal the wine we chose was a bottle of Chardonnay from Burgundy and found it seemed to be lasting us thirsty connoisseurs much longer than usual. I had forgotten from our visit last year that the house wines here were served in litres. Never mind, we coped with the extra. The house wines here are excellent and from named sources which you generally find is rarely the case.

The ambiance was brilliant and everyone was having a great time as madam gently served everyone with her usual efficiency and the aromas in the place were very French and continued to filter down from the tiny kitchen. Yet more garlic butter soaked snails passed our table. These the Japanese particularly seem to love. It is a pity that not more French people eat here but I suspect they cannot get a table. Quite late on in the evening at around 9.30 a tres, tres chic young French couple arrived to see if they could be fed. No tables were free as yet but madam said they could come back half an hour later at 10 and she would give them a table. Does she never sleep? – they also do lunch service as well. The pampered young lady of the couple looked very unamused and her partner was clearly being made to suffer for not getting her to a restaurant earlier. They duly arrived back at 10 and seated, once again the young lady had a face like thunder. She softened slowly and as the food arrived I think he was partially forgiven – possibly.

Paris is great for people watching.

We said our thankful goodbyes with kisses all round and a promise to return, hopefully next year.

The short stroll home with the floodlit views down the river was a very contented one and another memorable evening on this trip that had started early in the morning at the other end of France in Perpignan.

Saturday 24th September

Our first breakfast was a pleasant but strangely shambolic affair. Undeniably lovely staff manning the small breakfast room but they seemed thoroughly detached and concerned solely with keeping their area tidy rather than attending to the guests. Lots of smiles but there was no - 'what would you like to drink?' etc... Everything you required had to be asked for and they seemed oblivious to the milk or juice running out, I couldn't quite fathom out as to why they were all there. Being English, I asked for some milk to go with the tea, used it for the first cup and then someone else asked for the same and so they came and took ours and gave it to the other couple.

Very unusual service, or lack of it. Still they did keep smiling though.

Taking the only way out we ran past reception and out into the Rue Rivoli but still saw that our friend behind the frontier post was grinning from ear to ear as we went swiftly past him. I am starting to wonder if I had forgotten my trousers so just checked to make sure. If I thought for one moment that we were this funny we would have gone on the stage as a double act.

Again it is a beautiful cloudless morning in Paris and we are out early and the city is quiet and calm, but surely not for very long. We headed down the Rue Rivoli and then moved onto the right bank taking us as far as the Louvre and walked through the grand passageway towards the glass pyramid.

There is a pleasant early morning ambiance at the cafe overlooking the courtyard of the Louvre and we stroll through the imposing space over towards the Pont des Arts. There are still very few people on the streets and as we walk across the Pont des Arts we find ourselves  stopping to look at the amazing sight of all the engraved padlocks fixed to the metalwork and glistening in the strong sunlight.

These were not here on our visit last year as far as I recall and whoever it was who started this new 'tradition' of sealing your love onto this famous bridge I don't know but it is now nearly at full capacity and the bridge will probably fall into the Seine under the weight of them all if any more are put on. They have already started on other bridges, especially behind Notre Dame. We stand close to a young Italian couple who had just got engaged to be married and she was proudly showing off her ring as her partner attached their padlock to the bridge, but it was consumed by all the others. I suspect that there will be many more additions this weekend.

We walked on the left bank of the river for a while and got caught up amongst a large party of Polish tourists and struggled to escape the encirclement. When we  finally did we crossed the busy road but so did they and I nearly thought it would be easier just to join the tour.

We lost them eventually as we went back across to the bank of the river and as we did so I saw a young girl attempting reasonably successfully the - 'Is this your ring?' scam on a lady tourist. I went over and told the lady to just give the ring back and ordered the girl to 'allez'. I cannot believe people are still falling for this one.

Reaching the Musee D'Orsay we decided to visit as we discovered that they are closed Monday, the day we were hoping to go. Unfortunately they were redeveloping the dedicated Impressionist rooms so some of those pictures would not be on view. The advertised Oscar Wilde era exhibition would prove an excellent compensating diversion.

The queue outside the entrance was quite long but moved quickly and we went through the security checks. I had put my camera around the security sensors, placing it just behind some items belonging to the tourist in front of me. As he picked up his rucksack from the tray he somehow lassoed my camera. I watched with some alarm as it swung in apparent slow motion through the air loosely attached to the strap on his bag. I shouted at him and fortunately he saw what had happened and managed to lower his bag close to the floor before my camera fell off from about two feet off the ground. He was very apologetic and apart from a small chip it appeared to be OK. Fortunately, especially as I didn't know the Swedish for 'I am going to sue you'.

This museum is fabulous. The layout is very 'user friendly' and it never seems to get too crowded and the great thing about it having been built in a past life as a mainline train station is the abundance of natural light that comes flooding in.

What an incredible range of art there is here and we particularly love the paintings of the Impressionists and it is a special treat to see them up close and 'in the flesh' as it were. To us they are masterpieces and we wonder how these artists, who in the main had a lifelong struggle to get any attention, would have felt if they had known the interest shown and stratospheric value in their work today.

There are as we suspected a few Impressionist paintings unavailable to view but we are well satisfied with the visit. The 'Oscar Wilde' exhibition is perhaps stretching that description a bit. It is mainly art nouveau period pieces, art, furniture and costumes but it is a very fine and extensive display and really interesting despite the tenuous connection to the Irish writer. It conveys that particular lifestyle choice of the turn of the century period extremely well and the art etc.. stands up very well in comparison with the main collections in the museum.

Due to the renovations food choices are very limited so after about 2.5 hours we leave and get a bite to eat outside on the concourse. This space filled with tourists is of course full of the usual lively African traders trying to sell impossibly naff objects. I can only assume that somebody must buy them. The other product that is most popular with these vendors is bottled water at 'great' prices. We were laughing thinking about the classic episode of 'Only Fools and Horses' (hope you have seen this as I need to mention it again later – Google if not English) where Del Boy has the idea of bottling tap water in spring water bottles and making a fortune on it. I can't help thinking something similar is going on here – or am I just cynical?

We walk back towards the Place de la Concorde from the right bank by going over the Pont de la Concorde and stop to admire the wonderful views down both lengths of the river.

Paris looks absolutely wonderful today – at its atmospheric best. Hordes of people are enjoying themselves along the quays, sitting, strolling or fishing and the Seine river boats are packed with passengers and the lingering sounds betray that they are carrying increasingly lively crowds – the wine is flowing.

The Place is one of the great sights of Paris, wide, busy and lined with all its magnificent and very familiar architecture. It also has to be pointed out that it is very difficult to cross in safety. I especially wanted to get over to the Quay de la Concorde where there is one of the many moving memorials to those men and women who were killed during the last days of the liberation of Paris during August 1944. This one is particularly fascinating and intriguing. You will have read the more detailed account earlier in the book. I first came across this plaque in 2007 and thought the French wording unusual as it seemed to indicate that one of the two men who were 'executed' by the Germans at that spot actually survived.

Someone had placed flowers in front of the memorial just prior to our visit today and it is a reminder that there is more emotion to be found in Paris than just the romanticism of the city. The history of it, particularly the occupation history, I find really interesting and feel you get more out of a city if you do some research on its place in time.

We managed to avoid the onrushing traffic – how terrifyingly wide the Place looks when you are in the middle of it and about six rows of traffic are bearing down on you from their Le Mans starting grid. It was a relief to get back over to the gates of the Tuileries, a public garden that is Niamh's very favourite location in Paris. The gardens were incredibly busy with people enjoying the warm sunshine but we still managed to find a couple of the ubiquitous green chairs close to the lavender beds located at the foot of the curving ramp leading up to the Orangerie. It was certainly very hot, unseasonably so, and we must have stayed there overlooking the pool for a good hour relaxing and taking in the atmosphere, people watching as they all promenade to and from the Louvre. There are a lot of young people out today, many seem to be on a school or college organized trip. They are high spirited but good natured and well behaved and add colour to the extremely pleasant atmosphere.

I suggest an ice cream would go down well so off I go with Niamh's order. Four hours later (I exaggerate!) I returned the Italian ice cream stand near the fountain with two  wonderful tubs of delicious ice cream – but what a queue that was. It is an especially fine and lucrative business to be engaged in today.

This is all very pleasant, to be sat in the Tuileries near the fountain eating a superb ice cream in the late hot September sunshine. I do wish we could bottle the moment for recollection in deep mid- winter back home in the cold of England.

We eventually give up our seats to a grateful couple and move off to stroll down the wide promenade towards the Louvre, a wonderful spacious gravelled walk up the centre of the Tuileries. It is still bustling with happy throngs enjoying some glorious sunshine in this most perfect of settings. The cafes are fully occupied with contented customers and from my experience of sitting there last year I know they are making substantial profits on 'coffee with a view'.

At the far end of the walk we again have the Eiffel Tower sellers still trying very hard to dispose of their extensive stocks - but how do you get a two foot tower in your hand luggage? The Japanese seem to be the customers of choice to target and many thousands of Japanese dining rooms must have this particular decoration centre stage on the dining table.

Tiring a little in the heat we head back down Rue Rivoli to the hotel for a refreshing shower before heading out for the evening in search of a restaurant

On our arrival our friend the receptionist chuckles uncontrollably at our bedraggled state, unable to even utter 'bonjour'.

Refreshed and creeping under the eye-line of our nemesis we stroll into the heart of the Marais but soon get a bit indecisive about where we are to eat tonight. We sit for a while in the crowded square Place du Marche Sainte Catherine, a square that is bustling with diners and couples having a pre-dinner drink. Quite a number are families with young children, whom they are watching as they run excitedly around the square, sometimes having to quickly leave their aperitif and catch them as they run towards the quiet through road. One of the restaurants we were tentatively looking at was Les Bougresses on Rue de Jarente but we aren't sure about this one as it is still deserted despite its excellent rating on T/A.

We decided to wander back to the area around our Hotel and try to get in at Don Giovanni Italian restaurant at the rear of our hotel. When we get there it is also empty but we notice there are no menus of any description on view whereas last night there was a full menu and specials board.

I go in and have a word with the waiter but he says that they have a special party in tonight so there are no tables until about 9.30. That is too late for us so we walk back to Les Bougresses which proves not to have been the best dining decision I ever made. It will be an OK meal though even in our indecision we could have done better - but the people watching was a good compensation.

When we arrive at the restaurant it still has no occupied tables but we tentatively go in. Two men looking for all the world like a couple of hip-hop rappers are standing furtively behind a serving hatch at the far end of the restaurant. I go up to the first one and he seems like a rabbit caught in the headlights, I assume he must think I am from French immigration. He doesn't seem to speak any French, well certainly not Lancastrian French, and absolutely not a word of English.

My instincts are to run for the exit and select another dining experience but as we turn on our heels to leave a pleasant young lady comes through the front door into the restaurant and warmly invites us to select a table – not difficult as the choice is limitless. We are hungry and it does have a good reputation so we decide to stay, somewhat against my better judgement. We settle to just have a main and dessert course and when we begin to eat the first course - mine is roast lamb and Niamh has fish of the day, we are still the only diners in a sea of empty tables. From then on the restaurant starts to slowly fill up and by the time our dessert arrives amazingly all tables are taken.

The food on offer is decent but very simply presented; in fact most mains on the tables seem to be served with the same accompaniment, a rather bland and unusual version of potato mash. I think it has crushed butter beans folded through it but Niamh is doubtful. An unusual combination all the same. Desserts again are simple but these are enjoyable and the house rosé wine was of a good standard and fairly priced.

The first people to eventually enter the dining room after ourselves were a party of Australians that came to sit at the next table to us. Now, I generally do find that Australians are often quite gregarious but they were ensconced in their own little bubble and did not interact with their surroundings at all. Really this was the overall problem with this restaurant and perhaps that had something to do with the slightly diffident service. Unfortunately there wasn't an atmosphere or ambiance of note that was created at all and you felt that you were just being fed, meaning there was no other dimension to the evening which was a pity. That is until opposite us came to be seated a middle aged American couple hailing (loud hailing actually) from New York and I found it hard to take my eyes off them. I tried to listen with my super sensitive hearing which in view of her decibel levels was not overly used. This guy's wife never stopped talking, pausing only very briefly as food entered her mouth which just gave herself enough time for the fork to clear her lips. Her poor husband's head just got lower and lower to the table. She would be included in one of those groups of people for whom learning the word 'bonjour' is most certainly a step too far. She insisted on talking to the two young front of house staff totally in English, very verbally and loud, with no allowance for the fact that they obviously had very little comprehension of anything she was expounding.

She kept going on and on about her allergies and every time they brought anything to the table they got a long lecture about its possible contents and the consequences for her constitution. After one particularly strident discourse the young lady serving her turned around and pulled a face and sighed loudly and I had a job to keep a straight face. For the next visit she sent the young man to the table and it was funny to watch him shove the plate on the table, keep his head firmly down and run back to the kitchen before she could speak. At the start of the meal she desired a glass of rosé wine as an aperitif, but what a performance she surrounded that simple request with. I could see from the bottle on offer that they were proffering her a decent glass of French wine but she inevitably wasn't so sure. Sipping it again and again she then asked her husband for his opinion.

He was exasperated and just said tersely - 'its fine'.

'I suppose' she said, placing it reluctantly back on the table.

It was only an aperitif not a bottle of Chateau Petrus! So, in the end it was an entertaining session of people watching but not the best evening ever spent in a Paris restaurant.

The night, i.e. the time between then and breakfast, was notable for an incident that I am still not sure whether I should be proud of or simply just mortified about what occurred. I am really not sure quite what it says about me but here goes. The time was I suppose around 3am, a time that it has to be said my faculties are not generally at their sharpest as a rule. I sort of realised I was awake and to my horror there was a clear sound of movement behind the full length window curtain of the hotel room. To my ears there was also the unmistakable sound of the window being opened.

Now I do remember and I am in fact often reminded of the occasion just shortly after we were married when the menacing sound of the buzzing of a large bee was heard in our bedroom early one morning. My brave and instantaneous reaction was to leap from the bed and out of the room pulling the door tightly shut behind me, locking Niamh inside of course. I can't say I am really a man to face danger squarely in the face.

However, on this occasion my reaction was inexplicably so very different from that cowardly escape from raging insect terror. I leapt once again from the bed but instead of this time running for the door I without any thought for my personal safety pounced on the curtain and the shadowy form lurking behind that must have entered through the opened window. Grabbing the culprit in a vice-like grip there was a piercing scream that must have penetrated far into the still night time air of sleeping Paris.

I had the intruder secure in my grip but realised I would have to accept that we must come face to face and remove the curtain from between us. The reality of the situation hit home and I was now genuinely terrified at the prospect. Was the person armed in any way and how do we resolve this without injury?

The yellow light from the courtyard shone through the window as the curtain was ripped back and there in front of me and still in my grip was the miscreant – Niamh.

It was a balmy night and she had only got out of bed to open the window for some fresh cool air. However, in my defence she now knew that when the crunch came I would protect her from whatever the danger may be. Her more practical view was that I should have checked the contents of the bed first before bounding into action.

As I intimated I think only a bit of therapy might offer the correct interpretation of my eager impulsive actions.

Sunday 25th September

After another self-service breakfast amongst the gaggle of impotent staff we head out into the city with a cheery bonjour to our friend who finds that quip side-splittingly funny. We are eager to have a stroll around the Marais area as it is usually lively on a Sunday and so we walk towards the Place des Vosges. It doesn't take us long to decide that the sun is just too hot this morning and that getting nearer to the river would be a better option and so we walk across to the far end of the Islands. Today the L'Isle St Louis is very atmospheric in the early Sunday morning and we take our time to stroll through and take in the ambiance, a soft light filling the warm street, looking again at potential restaurants for tonight.

Considering that it is at the centre of the tourist areas this island has some lovely food shops and still retains its community feel which is a very large part of its attraction. It is an area that has not sold out to the tourists. Especially attractive is a superb cheese shop close by well-presented butchers/deli display – it is a pity we are not self-catering.

Eventually we make our way across the joining bridge to Notre Dame and even at this relatively early hour the surrounds of the Cathedral are heaving with tourists with a large snaking queue for the tower and a fair scrum of people jostling to get inside the cathedral itself. We are cornered (again) by a group of French boy scouts selling their scout calendar for the coming year. One breaks off from his friends and asks me to buy one but I explain that I have no use for it really. After he turns away I relent and go across and give him a donation as long as I don't get a calendar. They are so polite and it is a pleasure to see them doing something constructive in marked contrast to the pervading youth climate back in England.

I do generalise of course but in the main there is a noticeable difference in the respectfulness and dress code of the French children compared to what we see at home in the town where I work. That is reflected in the children's clothes shops here in France that would not stand a chance of staying open if they started a branch in England. Quantity before quality can be the standard back home.

Anyway before I start sounding like a 'Daily Mail' columnist we shall move on but not before we sit down on a bench in the square to admire the marvel that is Notre Dame.

After a minute or two a couple sit next to us, T-shirted with non- matching shorts and tattooed. Oh No! English, forgetting temporarily that so are we. What follows has to be one of the best arguments for not allowing just anyone to get a passport. There really should be a suitability test. I have to revert to 'Del boy' character again so if you are not English and it means nothing then once again I apologize. This time you have to think Boycie and Marlene and I kid you not.

The woman says (unbelievably) 'What they on about, that Notre Dame ain't on no island Boycie' (she didn't say Boycie though)

'Naw Marlene, it's just the way it looks on the river.'

We shuffle off the end of the bench and move away before we all get arrested and forcibly deported on the next ferry and walk across to the left bank of the Seine. I toss a coin into the box of the Tutankhamun impersonator in front of the fountain at St Michel and take a photo. One of the many guided walking tours of Paris has gathered there at the start of the trip and an over eager young man is trying to 'bond' this group of reluctant strangers by saying; 'and now for a bit of an icebreaker session'. Please, no - escape while you can.

With no wish to join in the forced sociability we head on down Rue St Andre. This is an atmospheric street for photography with many typically Parisian restaurants and is home to the vintage passage that leads to the old restaurant La Procope on the Rue de l'Ancienne Comedie and I spend a bit of time absorbing it all and taking some shots.

Walking back towards the river along the Rue de Seine we are stopped in our tracks by a large black shiny new Mercedes that pulls up just alongside of us.

A young impossibly stunning African girl steps out. I hope she wasn't looking at us too much as it was impossible not to be transfixed and just stare. 'Supermodel' doesn't begin to do justice to her appearance. The closest approximation I can offer in conjuring up this vision would be a young Iman, David Bowie's wife. She gracefully glides into a building opposite and I  think I may just have possibly noticed her six foot legs as she did so. I don't know who she was but from looking at her and her haute couture clothes and her expensively dressed and accessorised chauffeur/minder she was probably 'somebody'.

We finally reach the Pont des Arts and sit for a while absorbing the leisurely Sunday atmosphere. A young couple came to a section of the bridge close to us, he dressed in a white suit with red shoes and shirt and she in her white wedding dress. They attach a lock to the bridge and take a video with a passer-by helpfully making sure they also have a shot of each other. This is obviously becoming THE thing to do when getting engaged or married in Paris.

While this tender romantic event is going on a French singer is coming along the bridge making a video with his entourage, he is walking slowly down the Pont des Arts singing to the music being provided by the camera crew. I assume he is famous but unfortunately the last French singer to be known in England was probably Charles Aznavour.

When he has finished his lip syncing performance he swaggers confidently over to the newly married couple to offer his most 'sincere' congratulations with the fawning camera crew filming it all. He clearly expects to be recognized. He isn't. Kind of him though.

It is getting very close to lunchtime and so we make our way back to the Islands via the right bank of the river to listen to the accordionist on the Pont Neuf, grateful that he too wasn't singing.

From there we go down the steps to the small park area located at the tip of L'Isle de la Cite. You feel quite secluded here at a lower level than the island and you have a close up view of the tourist boats on the Seine as they pass by and an iconic view of the left bank. This is a timeless part of Paris that cries out for some black and white photography. It is filled with people having picnic lunches and the views over the river are excellent, boats passing on either side with the guided commentary drifting over on the breeze, clinking glasses almost drowning it out. We go back up the steps and stop by the accordionist again – this could only be Paris on a Sunday. From there we enter the Place Dauphine. The cafes and restaurants are already very busy and the outside tables are almost all taken. A large party of around twelve people are negotiating tables but it looks hopeless, this is not the time to be in Paris as a large group sans reservations. I don't think I have ever seen the city quite so busy. We stroll through the square, although, you could argue that it is more of a triangle shape, intending to go over to the L'Isle St Louis. Walking along the quay we get near to the Pont St Louis passing the atmospheric side streets leading the eye back to Notre Dam. We come to a very inviting cafe on the quayside that temptingly has an unoccupied table outside on the pavement. With a different and rather more tuneful accordion player on the bridge and the sun streaming onto the small terrace we find the atmosphere totally irresistible and it proves to be a highlight of our stay in Paris.

The atmosphere is very laid back, a young lady sat at the table behind us is leisurely picking at her food, her fork elegantly and nonchalantly balanced over her thumb while she continues to read a fashion magazine. An older French couple next to us are silently enjoying their  lunch and refilling their wine glasses from a carafe of red wine. A few more diners arrive but they have to sit inside and a couple of young Japanese tourists who have grabbed an outside table as it is vacated are asked to move inside because of only wanting to sit with a coffee.

The menu is light, mainly salads and quiche with wine by the carafe. We both have the smoked salmon quiche with salad and a carafe of rosé. All is well with the world, a really lovely lunch in surely one of the most relaxing spots in Paris. What a bonus to have the Paris 'soundtrack' drifting on the breeze from the bridge. Perfect!

As we admire the view there is a slight delay before the waiter takes our dessert order. We quite fancy ordering the same ones as the French couple - fromage blanc and an apple tart. Still no order is taken from us but our friendly waiter approaches carrying two apricot tarts and sets them down in front of us. A young couple father down the terrace, diners who I thought had previously ordered dessert are also still waiting so we assume we may have their desserts. The French couple next to us are laughing and I just say and gesture - 'quelle surprise'. We eat them anyway and they are very good and we order a finishing coffee. A very memorable Sunday lunch in Paris.

The cost is amazing, just 24 euros in total.

I find this a bit hard to believe but pay and leave a good tip. We leave the restaurant and the waiter follows us and is apologetic in admitting that he hasn't charged for the coffee. I give him the 4 euros and ask him if he has charged for the wine as I still think we have had a very good deal. He says yes so we are all very happy.

We go off to have a little siesta in the park at the end of the Island behind Notre Dame and we are feeling very chilled out. Many other people have had the same idea and this is a popular spot on a Sunday but we do find an empty bench to enjoy the early afternoon ambiance. The music of Paris from the bridge still drifting over on the breeze.

The last time we were here there was a man 'exercising' his parrot – yes really - and although we had earlier passed a man on the island carrying two parrots there is no colourful bird show on offer today. After a few minutes a French party on a guided tour arrives and forms a group just across from us. One of the two guides is carrying an accordion. The other guide launches into an extended speech and soon many of this party are looking quite restless and bored and start looking elsewhere for interest. Still he goes on and on and eventually starts handing out song sheets. These musical guides try to rouse the assembled throng with a sing along but by now the interest of the party has completely gone and all you can hear is the guides playing and singing.

To our relief they finally finish, move on I assume to the next musical place of interest. I suspect there may be a few of the group who break off and go somewhere else on their own. A most unusual tour.

In this usually quiet and contemplative park is the Memorial des Martyrs de la Deportation, a place where we unfailingly make a point of paying our respects when we come to Paris. It is a very striking memorial but because the most emotive part is almost completely below ground level not many visitors to Paris really know that it is there.

The entrance on ground level has a large low granite wall carved with the name of the memorial.

As you descend the stairs to the memorial below you lose touch with any sense of being in Paris as the only possible view is solely of the waters of the Seine.

The sight of anything other than the river is deliberately blocked out - you really leave your tourist self at the entrance. This starkly atmospheric place takes you somewhere far removed from a long lunch and the pleasing atmosphere of a Parisian Sunday.

There are many references to the various Nazi camps but it is the long narrow tunnel designed to indicate infinity with thousands of small lights that is most affecting - each single one representing an individual deportee.

This area is deliberately claustrophobic and stark, the walls have names of specific camps and moving words and poems by French writers and poets. The space down below also contains ashes from the camps in urns placed at both ends of the infinity light tunnel. An eternal flame burns and this is a place for contemplation and tears - I defy you not to be moved.

It is an incredibly affecting location, below and seemingly unknown by the tourist photographing Notre Dame or taking selfies just yards from the entrance. Our appreciation goes to De Gaulle for being brave enough to inaugurate this  monument many years before the powers that be and regrettably much of the population in France acknowledged their country's role in being complicit in this horrific, incomprehensible event.

At the entrance is comprehensive information about the deportations that heartbreakingly took place right up to the very final days before the liberation of Paris.

As the uprising in Paris took hold in August 1944 attempts, some successful, were made to derail and obstruct the train departures.

When you are one that personally qualify to have worn one of the coloured triangles that denoted the status of the deportees then this is a moving and reflective place to be as the reality hits home.

As we emerged back into the light I spoke in French to the young girl who was looking after the memorial, explaining why it personally affected us so much and thanked her for being there and remembering these people. I could tell that for her it was genuinely important to be a part of this commemorative site.

We strolled slowly and silently over to the bridge and suddenly the accordion player made sense even more. We stood for a while looking back over the river and Niamh at last managed to speak after drying her eyes and asked rhetorically why this simple structure had such an effect on her. It had to be rhetorical for I couldn't answer as I still couldn't bring myself to utter a word and was looking away, lost in thought.

Paris is a place to enjoy yourself but it is healthy and vital to be reminded that life has wider issues as well.

Composed once more, we moved off the bridge and onto the Island and the streets were incredibly busy with long, long queues for Bertillon's Ice cream. Is it the best in the world? Well we have a lovely one back home in Lancashire but Bertillon I have to say is pretty fine.

After having another peruse of the menus of the potential restaurants for this evening we find a bit of quiet solitude in the church of Saint-Louis-en-l'Île Church. This is well worth a visit and its history goes back prior to the French Revolution. You can imagine this may have been a place of refuge during that period. A surprise to find such a church on this street and a reminder this island is still very much a community and not just for us tourists.

We slowly make our way back to the hotel to freshen up and ironically in view of our visit to the memorial after our lunch we end up inadvertently going by the Jewish Shoah  Memorial. We walk along the long wall dedicated to the 'Righteous amongst the nations'. Directly across from that list of names grouped into the years when these courageous people were given that title is a school. This has a plaque telling us that most of its young occupants were deported never to return. This was such a poignant link to our time on the Islands and again a very moving place.

At our hotel for once and thankfully our receptionist is nowhere to be seen and we dash into the lift.

It will be our last evening meal of the trip tonight so we want it to be a memorable one.

We had more or less decided on Aux Anysetiers Du Roy on Rue St Louis en L'Isle, highly rated on T/A. I go in through the ancient doorway to enquire if they may have a table. Happily, they do and we sit down at a table, designed I think for Snow White and the seven dwarfs.

It has the most unusual chunky wooden chairs but these are small and close to the ground. They are not for a tall person that is for sure but we diminutive people are OK. It has to be said that the restaurant is unusual. It is almost medieval in theme and one side of the dining room to the right of our table is very dimly lit. We notice a party really struggling to read the menu.

A young man comes tentatively over with our menu. He is pleasant but seems a bit nervous and a little unsure of himself. We see why very shortly when the lady owner comes breezing through the restaurant. She clearly runs this place on very strict lines and you would not want to slip below the standards she clearly expects of her staff. During the evening she is everywhere, keeping an eye on proceedings and has an obvious uncompromising pride in her restaurant. Pity she can't source any light bulbs.

We order an exceptionally fine bottle of Sancerre (it is the last night) and just decide on a main and dessert. Niamh has salmon and it is really lovely, perfectly cooked and that is not always the case. I have the confit of duck with sauté potatoes which is as good as any I have ever had anywhere in France. Super main courses.

The desserts were equally up to a very high standard and with the excellent bottle of Sancerre it was an exceptional meal enjoyed in a most unusual quirky setting.

At the next table were an English couple who were just returning from an organized train journey through Italy and France with 'Great Rail Journeys'. It was interesting to talk with them as I had looked a few times at doing one of these tours but ultimately had never taken the plunge. From what they said the tour sounded very tiring and a little rushed and I think they as well as ourselves felt that we had done the train touring in the best possible way – by ourselves.

They were good company and added to our enjoyment of the evening and the restaurant does have a very pleasing but individual atmosphere. It comes highly recommended if a little out of our comfort zone as regards the setting.

We slowly meandered back to the hotel enjoying every last moment in this wonderful city on the last evening of our stay in Paris. With our later train times though we still had more or less a full day to come.

Monday 26th September

Sadly, as we would have so loved to say goodbye, our friend is not on duty today and we leave our bags with the lady on reception. We stroll along the Rue Rivoli as far as the Louvre and walk through the passageway to the glass pyramid. The cafe on the terrace is just getting into breakfast service and it is altogether a totally different, relaxed atmosphere on this early Monday morning. The Tuileries gardens are peaceful and in complete contrast to what you would generally encounter on a weekend and we have a pleasant walk through to visit the Orangerie.

There is a small queue inside the foyer and we are behind an older American couple for whom any length of queue is clearly a major international incident. Over the top or what. He keeps going to the front checking out the reason for the unbearable three minute delay, she is leaning on the wall doing stretching exercises and he re-joins her and does the same. What a performance and they are very disdainful and rude to the girl when they get to the front. Chill out will you, this is supposed to be a pleasure.

The two Monet Galleries are calm and a feast for the senses. What amazing paintings these are and you can only wonder at the quantity of  oils needed to finish them. We sit for a while taking them in and I take a few photos, sneaking my camera into operation as the fussy security guard moves out of view. Unlike the Musee D'Orsay you can, despite what this man decides is his personal local bylaw, take pictures in here and downstairs in the gallery containing the Renoirs, Cézannes etc.. I make full use of this opportunity. If you have never been around this gallery then don't miss it next time you are here – it is breathtakingly wonderful.

We go back through the Tuileries for one last

time and head over to the L'Isle St Louis and the Café Med. We pass through the Place Dauphine and go round by the left bank quay. Coming to the Prefecture de Police it is worth looking up at the building. There is still plenty of evidence of the final days of the occupation in 1944 when it was the centre of action, the focus of the now unstoppable uprising. Unrepaired bullet holes still pockmark the exterior and again as so often when strolling around Paris it is difficult to visualize a time when it was not as peaceful as we find it today.

Cafe Med as usual is simply a delight. Uncomplicated cooking, well executed and amazing value. Madam with her shock of blonde hair is not on duty today but her deputies are pleasant and efficient. An arrogant young couple come in and want to sit at the large table but the young girl politely asks them to take a table for two. They decline without grace and leave in a strop. It is their loss. How can you get yourself in such a mood in this city?

A smartly dressed young man comes to sit next to us, clearly he is on his lunch break from the office. He sits quietly, slowly eating his way through the cheapest menu and drinks only tap water, comfortable in his own space. This you would never see in England, young people would probably snatch a MacDonald's or a Subway roll and certainly would never think of having a quiet hour alone in a restaurant eating a three course set menu. Come to think of , there is a reason for that - you would never find such a restaurant.

We leave well satisfied and have a last meandering stroll on the Islands before heading back to the hotel to collect our bags. With plenty of time to spare we decided to walk to the Gare de Nord. It is an interesting and educating walk to say the least as we make our way up the long Boulevard de Sébastopol, a street which changes markedly in character as you get nearer to the station.

Going through the African quarter it really feels wise to just keep your head down and head on quickly. It is an experience though and certainly another side to this fascinating city. We pass a few men barbecuing meat in stolen shopping trolleys. Love to see that catch on back in the UK. They are doing a brisk trade though and I can't see any police around here ready to stop them.

And that is it. The journey back to Preston is uneventful and easy. A wonderful trip and the memories will once again get us through the winter.

IS PARIS MORE BEAUTIFUL IN THE RAIN?

This feels like a good subject to end on although I have a feeling I will be writing more about Paris in the future – the story is not fully told nor has it ended. At the end of 'Midnight in Paris' Gil and his new love Gabrielle head off to a new beginning as they walk across the Seine on Pont Alexandre III unconcerned by the falling rain. In fact to them 'Paris is more beautiful in the rain'. Whether Hemingway ever shared the same romantic vision of Paris we do not know though somehow I doubt that he did.

So, the question remains – Is Paris more beautiful in the rain? I can say that I am a considerable authority on the matter as I have been caught in many a heavy downpour in the city. Paris is quite an open city and it is really a matter of chance as to whether you may find any shelter. That may also cloud your judgement on the matter. The rain does certainly offer a different perspective in Paris and the city changes in character more than anywhere else I have been when the streets and probably you are very wet.

The first time we were caught in the rain was on the Champs-Élysées and the downpour came on very suddenly. We were crossing over, a difficult manoeuvre at the best of times, from Ladurée to the opposite side when the heavens opened. By the time we had crossed and hid beneath a tree we were extremely wet. Strangely though it did not seem to matter to me and with my photographer's eye I felt compelled to reach for my camera and capture the moment. Niamh was not quite so enthusiastic and she ran across the pavement and into H & M. This was not quite so romantic as she can go in an H & M store anywhere but I stayed to watch the rain on the street. I captured a moment and it was one of my favourite shots of Paris.

So it was so far so good as regards my feeling about the rain in Paris – it looked atmospheric to me that day. I caught up with Niamh who was standing in a small puddle of water in H & M and she was unimpressed.

Niamh was equally unimpressed the second time we got a Paris soaking. On arrival at the Gare du Nord the weather was grey but mild and fine. I suggested that as we were early we could walk to our hotel located just off the Rue Rivoli. We were near the Hotel de Ville when the cloud burst came and my reputation for forecasting the weather was shattered. As we came into the square a loud commotion started up. All we could see was a throng of people in the square holding placards, shouting and blowing horns at ear splitting decibels. Police were manoeuvring them quite roughly towards one corner of the space and right past where we had entered the square. We wisely stepped back but there was no cover from the rain and also no way of retreating or going forward.

After what seemed an age we managed to sneak behind the last line of police and away down the side of the square and threaded our way to our hotel and a hot shower. Not a terribly romantic moment.

Soaking number three was one I described earlier in the book when we emerged from Invalides

Metro station to a very open air view of Les Invalides after a journey from Montmartre – not one of my better plans. As I recounted we ended up in Les Recruitment Café in a state of total dishevelment and I can say without hesitation that it was the wettest I have been fully clothed. The same applied to all the party I had led there. I did not ask them whether Paris was more beautiful in the rain.

The fourth time was more of a fine drizzle – if you are English you will be aware of the expression: 'you know - the fine stuff that wets you through'. To be honest it had been a bit of a miserable trip weather wise but we could not allow the elements to spoil our fun. The Tuileries are a must and even though the rain was gently falling we had to go to the gardens.

Just by the Musée de l'Orangerie we paused and looked at an extraordinary sight of the clouds coming down so low that two thirds or so of the Eiffel Tower had 'disappeared' giving the impression that it was still under construction. The view over the Place de la Concorde to the tower was an unmissable photo opportunity and a unique view of a familiar sight. Even Niamh was close to conceding that Paris could be more beautiful in the rain. Alas, we were again exceptionally moistened and ran to the Orangerie to dry out and enjoy once again Monet's masterpieces.

Finally our last major encounter with the Paris rain was on a later trip with friends. The weather for the most part had been excellent but on our last morning before heading back to the Gare du Nord it was a dark, wet and filthy day. The leaden skies looked set for the day, proper summer cricket weather as we English would reflect. Perhaps Niamh and I were beginning to get this 'Paris in the rain' thing. The others stayed at the hotel playing cards but we intrepid explorers decided that we were going out; not to be cheated out of our last day in Paris.

So that is what we did.

We were wet by the time we got to the Metro La Motte Picquet Grenelle and we stayed wet for our entire trip. We were safe under cover on Rue Rivoli sheltered by the street arcade and enjoyed the shops and cafés. We bought a touristy bag with Paris and Eiffel towers stamped all over it that we still have in use today. This helped to keep our purchases fairly dry as they were suffering in the damp conditions. Wetter still, we headed through the Tuileries for one last time and then back on the Metro to the hotel.

Our friends took one look at us and were incredulous that we were actually laughing and they despaired at our madness in going out in such a deluge. We though had finally got it - perhaps, just perhaps Paris is more beautiful in the rain.

Now it has to be said that I am not the best judge of this. I have lived most of my life in the North of England. I spent the first part of my life in the small town of Darwen, Lancashire. This is in a valley and was known for its cotton and paper mills that dominated the landscape. These are industries that need water, lots of water if you are following my drift. The town is overlooked from the moor above by a tower built to commemorate the diamond jubilee of Queen Victoria in 1897. There is a local saying that 'If you can't see the tower it is raining and if you can see it then it is going to rain'. That is a fairly accurate view of the Darwen weather.

So is Paris more beautiful in the rain? Well, I think you can see that I am clearly not the man to make the final judgement, my senses are impaired. You will just have to experience it for yourself.

If you have enjoyed my book please leave a review on Amazon where you will also find my other writings - available worldwide. Thank you for reading, I very much appreciate your interest and support.

All Available on Amazon for Kindle & Unlimited

NEW BOOK July 8th 2022

Or for something different - a Family History memoir

ABOUT THE AUTHOR

Neal Atherton

My passion is writing about travel and particularly French travel. I have traveled extensively in France and wine and food has always featured on my travels and now in my books. My friends always await our return from France with the latest new finds from the vineyards and I was more than happy to keep sampling. I am from  Lancashire in the north of England but have now relocated to Somerset (nearer to France) and able to enjoy devoting my time to writing and new discoveries.

France came late to me as a destination, in fact so conservative was my travel upbringing that it was a long time before I even ventured to Cornwall. I have more than made up for the slow start and have enjoyed helping many others with their travel plans to France and especially to Paris and Provence.

I have written a series of four books on France - Three are also on Amazon:THE FIRST TIME WE SAW PARIS about our first steps in French Travel, THYME FOR PROVENCE our discovery of that glorious region and the people and places we met and discovered, A DREAM OF PARIS a personal memoir of our times in Paris with friends.

France has been fun, we have been burgled on our very first arrival, we discovered the best cafe that changed our travel lives on the very next day, we learnt about French wine, we escaped from the most horrendous gite, we found the best of gites, B &

B's and people, we laughed and cried with dear friends in Paris, I was hosed down by a crazy owner to cool me down in Provence, our breakfast in a remote village was served by the French army, we stepped totally out of our comfort zone and discovered the best of French culture. The experiences are varied and many and please come with me as I retell the stories and my footsteps are there to follow.

I also write about ancestry and genealogy and my first book about our incredible family story themed around war and the military is now on Amazon - A BULLET FOR LIFE.

I love the English game of cricket, golf, soccer, photography, walking and cooking. Oh, and travel of course.

PRAISE FOR AUTHOR

Kindle EditionVerified Purchase re A Dream of Paris

'Found this well written and informative. Certainly gets the atmosphere of Paris and especially the gastronomic side of what Paris has to offer'

- AMAZON

First Time We Saw Paris
5.0 out of 5 stars Delightful
Reviewed in the United States on February 1, 2020
Format: Kindle EditionVerified Purchase
I so enjoyed the style of writing. It felt like I was there with you. It did inspire me with a desire to visit France and these places in particular. I would recommend this book to anyone who is thinking of a trip to France.

- AMAZON

Thyme for Provence
5.0 out of 5 stars Entertaining and very enjoyable
Reviewed in the United States on August 25, 2019
Format: Kindle Edition

BOOKS BY THIS AUTHOR

First Time We Saw Paris

Across the channel - a sense of wonder at seeing Paris for the first time - south on Autoroute du Soleil - Catalonia & the Mediterranean Sea - Innocents Abroad.
What did we find - what is France REALLY like?
We found a lifelong love of France BUT first ....
French travel has been fun, we were burgled on our very first night, we discovered the finest cafe that changed our travel lives the very next morning, we learned about French wine, we escaped the most horrendous gite, we found the best of gites, B & B's & people, we laughed and cried with dear friends in Paris, I was hosed down by a crazy owner to 'cool me down' in Provence, our breakfast was served by the French army, we stepped out of our comfort zone and discovered the best of French culture.

The experiences are many and varied and this is the first of four travel memoirs that tell the full story - PROVENCE is next - Please be with me from the start. - Please use the LOOK INSIDE feature

I will inspire you to find the most amazing places & people yourself in this wonderful land

For me it has been the most remarkable ride for a very reluctant traveller - Come with me

Thyme For Provence

'Monsieur, you are hot from the journey, oui?'
I could only agree that I was indeed the very picture of the Englishman in the noonday sun.
She broke away from watering her extensive and beautiful enclosed garden.
'I will cool you down'
Turning the hose on my fully clothed self she most certainly did that.

This is an affectionate account of our French travels in Provence - meeting so many remarkable (and eccentric) people and places over a 20 year period travelling by car from the North of England Is it a guide book? Well, the people and places are there but I really want to inspire you to make your own journey and treasure this gorgeous region.
If not, then be entertained from your armchair and let your imagination take you to the lavender fields in a great summer read

A Bullet For Life

Kimberley, South Africa - 1900
Saturday February 10th 1900 was another day under siege for James Atherton. He was serving with the Loyal North Lancashire Regiment engaged in defending Kimberley in South Africa and urgently in need of relief which came five days later. His friend on duty next to him was Samuel Hall from Preston in Lancashire, a town some 11 miles from James home in Darwen. The following day Samuel would be dead.
The friends had travelled to fight as professional soldiers together twelve months earlier and Samuel may also have been with James in Ceylon on his previous posting. The death of

Samuel was a crushing blow to James but on his return he visited Samuel's widowed mother Sarah now also living in Darwen. Sarah was born in Lisburn in Ireland and had settled with her husband William, a man from County Cork, now an Army pensioner.

It was here that he found love amongst the tragedy. Samuel's sister Lydia was 22 and they were married some two years later.

Did Lydia know of James troubled past?

Let us see but the ending returns to South Africa, via Spain, Cornwall, Cumbria, Ireland, France, Italy and Lancashire and spans two centuries - The ending is heartwarming in the most unexpected coming together of a family line in an amazing coincidence - Life truly does hang by a thread - or a bullet

This a story that has taken some 12 years of research and although it was fun to unravel all the complex details it was like most family research also at times frustrating and I conclude the book with some research tips that I trust will be helpful.

Made in the USA
Las Vegas, NV
27 August 2022

54142652R00135